SIMPLE MEAL SOLUTIONS *for* GLP-1 DIETS

This book is dedicated to those of us who still want to love and appreciate tasty food, despite all the times we've battled with it in our lives.

Quarto.com

First Published in 2026 by Fair Winds Press, an imprint of The Quarto Group,
100 Cummings Center, Suite 265-D, Beverly, MA 01915, USA.
T (978) 282-9590 F (978) 283-2742

EEA Representation, WTS Tax d.o.o.,
Žanova ulica 3, 4000 Kranj, Slovenia.
www.wts-tax.si

Fair Winds Press titles are also available at discount for retail, wholesale, promotional, and bulk purchase. For details, contact the Special Sales Manager by email at specialsales@quarto.com or by mail at The Quarto Group, Attn: Special Sales Manager, 100 Cummings Center, Suite 265-D, Beverly, MA 01915, USA.

30 29 28 27 26   1 2 3 4 5

ISBN: 978-1-57715-576-8

Digital edition published in 2026
eISBN: 978-1-57715-577-5

Library of Congress Cataloging-in-Publication Data available

Design and Page Layout: Megan Jones Design
Photography: WWH Media, LLC

Printed in Guangdong, China TT102025

The information in this book is for educational purposes only. It is not intended to replace the advice of a physician or medical practitioner. Please see your health-care provider before beginning any new health program.

SIMPLE MEAL SOLUTIONS *for* GLP-1 DIETS

75 Recipes for Sustainable Weight Loss and Good Health

Summer Kessel, RD, CSOWM, LDN

CONTENTS

Introduction

As a registered dietitian and a notoriously hungry gal who loves to eat tasty food, my approach to balancing nutrition with managing my weight has been a lifelong roller coaster. For nearly thirty years (to be clear, I'm only just turning forty!), I have *struggled* with the always-present, intrusive experience of food noise and with a massive appetite that resulted in my living in a much larger body than felt comfortable, healthy, or personally acceptable. Of course, I didn't understand what was happening to me as a teen, but if I hadn't been involved in sports, I just know I would have been much heavier in high school. During my college years, with less activity and unlimited access to food, I quickly packed on the pounds. To manage, I bought every cookbook. I tried every fad diet, quick fix, commercially available program, prescription medication, and exercise program I could get my hands on. I took cooking classes, I paid for meal plans, I had coaches, and I ate prepackaged foods. And every time, I would eventually encounter yet another round of disappointment and frustration. The cycle of dieting, losing, giving up, regaining, and starting over was *exhausting*.

I was so committed to figuring out how to manage my weight that I eventually pursued a second career as a registered dietitian. Surprise! Even that wasn't enough. Despite all the social, political, and environmental determinants of health (time, money, resources, education, support, access, mental health, and mobility) leaning in my favor, why did I have to work *so hard* to make any progress in losing weight? Why did healthy eating require such painstaking attention to detail? Despite knowing how to lose weight, how I should eat, how to move my body, and how to navigate my environment, why couldn't I get it done consistently enough to lose the weight? I have been a goal achiever throughout my life. I'm an amazing mother (if I do say so myself). I'm smart, funny, kind, and inclusive. I loved myself enough to want to take care of my health and my nutrition and my fitness. But I was just so hungry!

The *why* of my struggles became clear: Obesity is a disease. It's progressive, relapsing, recurring, and frankly, a pain in the ass to manage. Eventually and thankfully, I came to accept that my motivation, drive, and knowledge simply couldn't combat my biology. And it was okay to ask my doctor for more help. It wasn't until I started a GLP-1 (glucagon-like peptide-1) medicine that I began to truly realize it was never my fault. I have finally achieved the real and lasting changes I always wanted—not only in my weight but in my relationship with food, too! GLP-1 medicines have been a game changer for me. A revelation. A relief. A new chance. And so much more than just another fad or quick fix! Finally, with my appetite dysfunction and food noise in check, I can stick to my best intentions for good nutrition and lose weight in a way that doesn't suck. In fact, I have found more freedom to eat the foods I love because I can trust that I won't *overeat* them. Gone are the days of eating boring, simple meals and tracking every detail. Now I eat more intuitively while prioritizing the things that really matter—such as balance, protein, and fiber—without sacrificing taste or variety.

GLP-1 MEDICINES AND HOW THEY WORK

GLP-1 medications—such as Ozempic, Wegovy, Mounjaro, and Zepbound—are FDA-approved for use in managing both diabetes and obesity, and they have been monumental in changing the way the world thinks about weight loss. Despite what we may hear in sensationalized online content, these medications are safe and effective when used properly under the supervision and guidance of a medical professional, as all prescription medications should be.

The GLP-1 agonist medications are peptides that mimic the hormone GLP-1 to stimulate GLP-1 receptors all over the body, primarily in the gut, pancreas, brain, and heart. Although all humans produce naturally occurring GLP-1 hormone after we eat, which helps us regulate hunger, the hormone usually only survives in the body for a few hours. The pharmaceutical peptides stimulate the GLP-1 receptors continuously for about a week before "wearing off." The result? A prolonged and stable reduction (not elimination) of appetite. These medications dampen our cravings, enhance our brain's perception of satiety, and slow gastric emptying time so you feel fuller longer after eating reasonably balanced and nutritious meals. When taking one of these medicines, it becomes much easier to eat somewhat smaller portions, make generally healthier choices, and avoid the usual temptations of the calorie-rich food environment around us that often results in our overeating. The medications make it easier for us to decrease the overall calories we consume across all our meals and snacks, which drives the calorie deficit needed for weight loss. Usually, when trying to eat less, we feel hungrier—but not on these medicines. Eating less is no longer a misery-inducing endeavor!

To be super clear here, if you take away anything from reading this, let it be this: The goal of a GLP-1 medicine is not to make you eat as little as possible or never be hungry. It is to help people like me (and maybe you) who have big, difficult appetites now *feel* like those appetites are more manageable.

GLP-1 medications also improve insulin sensitivity. If you struggle with the very normal insulin resistance that often accompanies excess fat on the body, you can now appropriately metabolize carbohydrates for energy and more efficiently pull glucose into cells and muscles instead of having it linger in the blood (high blood sugar). Eating low-carb or keto or avoiding every sweet treat is no longer necessary. In fact, as you'll see throughout this book, carbohydrates are now a key part of the plan. (Yay!) This is of course why these medicines are highly effective in the treatment of diabetes, even if the person taking it doesn't lose much weight.

HOW I APPROACH FOOD AS A DIETITIAN AND PERSON WHO LOVES TO EAT!

Taking GLP-1 medicines and feeling like our appetite is less huge is only part of the equation. To truly thrive on these medicines, we need a realistic approach to nutrition and eating well that we can put into practice in our very real, busy, and complicated lives. Remember, good nutrition and health isn't just about being a certain weight. We still need to think about gut health, heart health, cancer prevention, our muscles, skin, and hair—and most importantly, *enjoying our food*!

In my many years on these medications and working as a registered dietitian with thousands of others who take them, I have developed a nutrition framework that prioritizes nutrient-dense whole foods in tasty, balanced meals. It's important to have realistic solutions to the challenges that can come with eating well while on these medicines. A truly sustainable weight-loss journey is one that prioritizes eating in a way you can see yourself doing for the rest of your life. That family dessert your grandma used to make? We're eating it! That traditional cultural food that connects you to your heritage? Hell yes. The meal that reminds you of your favorite vacation spot? Amazing! Eating well is not about eating perfectly, but instead having a plan for eating in a way that aligns with your goals and improves your quality of life. Your nutrition plan should serve you and support your goals even when life's conditions aren't perfect. Too busy to cook breakfast every day? We got you. A little nauseous at dinner? There are always options! The truth is, feeding ourselves is a skill that takes practice and problem-solving. Not a great cook? No worries, *me neither*, but together we're gonna figure it out!

This cookbook is about helping you build habits that last—not following rigid food rules or restrictive diets. Whether you're dealing with side effects, struggling to get enough protein, or just trying to find meals that work for you, these recipes provide practical solutions to help you feel your best. This is your journey, your body, and your health—let's make it work in a way that feels *good*.

WHY THIS COOKBOOK

This cookbook offers a collection of recipes and tips that have helped my patients and me eat well and feel our best! If you're using a GLP-1 medication, you've likely experienced shifts in your appetite, digestion, and even the way you think about food. Although these medications can be powerful tools for managing weight and metabolic health, they work best in combination with balanced, nourishing meals. That's where this cookbook comes in.

Our goal? To make eating on a GLP-1 medication *easy*, *delicious*, and *satisfying*—all while supporting your nutritional needs. The recipes in this book aren't about restriction. Instead, they focus on affordable, nutrient-dense meals that fuel your body, keep you feeling full and energized, and most importantly, taste incredible. Please know, this is not a "diet" book. It's a sustainable way of eating that works with your medication, lifestyle, and personal preferences. Whether you're a beginner cook or a seasoned home chef, these recipes are designed to be approachable yet exciting, using everyday ingredients that won't break the bank.

This book is organized into practical sections to fit every part of your day:

- **Breakfasts:** High-protein options to start your morning strong, even when nothing sounds good or you're short on time.
- **Lunches and dinners:** Balanced, satisfying, and flavorful meals that help you achieve your protein and fiber targets—and still taste great!
- **Snacks and treats:** Light options for when you need a little extra fuel between meals. This chapter also includes a few sweet treats that can satisfy the very normal cravings that may still linger while you're on a GLP-1 without derailing your progress.
- **Sips and beverages:** Nutritious, hydrating drinks that support your goals.

Every dish follows these guiding principles:

- They are **balanced** to include foods from all food groups in the ratios that support dietary diversity, flexibility, sustainable weight loss, and blood sugar management.
- They are **high in lean protein** (around 30 grams of protein per meal) to help preserve muscle mass, manage hunger, and keep you satisfied.
- They are **calorie smart** so you can eat within the calorie deficit your body needs for a steady and safe rate of weight loss but harness the energy you need to live your best life!
- They are **loaded with vegetables and fruits** (at least 1 cup per meal) to provide color, texture, variety, fiber, vitamins, minerals, and antioxidants.
- They **intentionally include smart carbohydrates** (½ to 1 cup of fiber-rich sources such as whole grains, beans, or starchy vegetables) for steady energy and for gut health.

- **Healthy fats** in moderation are sprinkled in to enhance flavor and support overall health without overloading on butter, oil, or cheese.
- The collection **leans into diversity** and includes a variety of cultural flavors and traditional foods so we can continue to appreciate the foods that bring us joy.
- **Accessibility and affordability** of cooking methods and ingredients are prioritized so that eating well doesn't have to break the bank or take up all your time.
- There is **transparency** into exact portion sizes, calories, and macronutrients for those who track the details. Plus, clear cooking instructions help you build confidence in the kitchen.

Sometimes GLP-1 medications slow digestion and dampen the appetite to such a degree that eating enough is hard! Smaller portions of nutrient-dense foods can go a long way when it is difficult to achieve our nutrition goals. You may feel full faster, and large, heavy meals might not sit well. That protein or vegetable target might feel overwhelming sometimes. That's why many of these recipes will also focus on:

- **Portion awareness** to offer right-sized servings that align with your reduced appetite without sacrificing nutrition.
- **Digestion-friendly ingredients** across the fiber spectrum to meet your gut wherever it may be on your journey. We have meals that are gentle on the stomach to help avoid discomfort and others that are rich enough to keep things moving.
- **Hydration and electrolyte balance** because staying hydrated can be tricky.
- **Gluten-free, vegetarian, and vegan dishes** so that even when there are foods we don't eat, we have options.

Eating well on a GLP-1 medication isn't just about following a meal plan—it's about navigating the unique challenges that come with your changing appetite, digestion, and taste preferences. This cookbook is designed to help you lose weight at a healthy rate while maintaining a positive relationship with food—without feeling like you're constantly "on a diet." Many traditional weight-loss approaches focus on restriction, but that mindset isn't sustainable. Instead, these recipes help you eat in a way that fuels your body, supports your goals, and feels enjoyable.

CHAPTER 1

Understanding GLP-1 Nutrition

GLP-1 medicines are not magic. They are powerful tools that, when combined with a thoughtful nutrition plan, can lead to remarkable health improvements. A nutrition plan that supports an enjoyable and healthy journey on GLP-1 medicines is one that prioritizes whole, unprocessed foods such as fruits, vegetables, lean proteins, whole grains, and healthy fats in the form of adequate and balanced meals. These foods not only provide essential nutrients but also help keep you feeling full and satisfied, which is key when you're trying to manage your weight. These medicines work best by keeping you fuller longer on smaller, healthier meals. But to feel that satisfaction, you have to eat *enough*! Instead of restricting food to drive weight loss, your job is to think about how you will fuel your body and care for it in a way that promotes great long-term health.

The Nutritional Role of Each Food Group

Every ingredient in this cookbook is chosen with purpose: to help you lose weight at a healthy rate, support muscle mass, manage side effects, and keep you feeling satisfied. Let's break down the key nutritional benefits of each component and why they matter, especially while you are on a GLP-1 medication.

PROTEIN: THE FOUNDATION OF EVERY MEAL

Protein is essential for preserving muscle mass, supporting metabolism, and promoting satiety—all crucial factors in sustainable weight loss. Because GLP-1s reduce appetite, it's easy to under-eat protein, which can lead to muscle loss instead of fat loss. Proteins are the body's building blocks, vital for growth and repair. They play a critical role in the structure, function, and regulation of tissues and organs and are integral in forming enzymes, hormones, and antibodies, making them essential for immune function, muscle growth, and tissue repair. Proteins are composed of amino acids, some of which are essential, meaning we must obtain them through our diet. Each gram of protein provides approximately 4 calories.

Determining the right amount of protein to consume is important and varies based on several factors, including age, sex, physical activity level, and overall health. The USDA recommended dietary allowance (RDA) for protein generally stands at 0.8 grams of protein per kilogram of body weight for the average adult. This, however, has been debated; it may be much too low for most people.

For those individuals looking to achieve or maintain weight loss (and those who engage in regular physical activity), the requirement is much more—between 1.2 and 2.0 grams of protein per kilogram of body weight to support muscle repair and growth and to keep you fuller longer. Of course, that 2.0 g/kg may be unreachable at our higher starting weights, especially if your appetite is suppressed. But you should be able to slowly work your way up closer to the high end of the range the closer you get to a healthy weight.

Note: A moderately high protein intake—as recommended here—is safe for healthy individuals with normal kidney function.

GLP-1s get a bad rap for increasing the risk for muscle loss. This is a risk with any method of weight loss, but it is important to try to preserve as much muscle as possible to support your metabolic health and chances of long-term weight-loss main-tenance. Rest assured, a high-protein diet paired with regular resistance training does the trick.

THE BEST SOURCES OF PROTEIN

- **Lean meats and poultry (e.g., chicken, turkey, lean beef):** high-quality, low-fat protein
- **Fish and seafood (e.g., salmon, shrimp, cod, tuna):** provide omega-3s for heart and brain health
- **Eggs and dairy (e.g., Greek yogurt, cottage cheese, low-fat cheese):** protein-packed and gut-friendly
- **Plant-based proteins (e.g., tofu, tempeh, beans, lentils):** great alternatives when meat isn't appealing
- **Protein powders and shakes:** convenient options when solid food is hard to eat

CARBOHYDRATES: SMART ENERGY FOR SATIETY AND PERFORMANCE

Carbs fuel your body and brain, but choosing high-fiber, slow-digesting carbs is key for steady energy and reduced cravings. Because GLP-1s slow digestion, the right types of carbs can help prevent blood sugar crashes and provide lasting energy.

Often referred to as the body's primary energy source, carbohydrates, such as those found in whole grains, rice, potatoes, pasta, and oats, are important for fueling daily activities. When consumed, carbohydrates break down into glucose, which is then used by the body's cells to produce energy. Each gram of carbohydrate provides about 4 calories.

Carbohydrates can be broadly categorized into simple (sugars) and complex (starches and fibers). Simple carbohydrates, or simple sugars, consist of one or two sugar molecules and are quickly absorbed by the body. Examples include fructose, glucose, and sucrose found in candies, fruits, and processed foods. They provide rapid energy but can lead to spikes and crashes in blood sugar levels. Although simple carbohydrates provide quick bursts of energy, complex carbohydrates offer a more sustained release, contributing to long-term energy maintenance. Complex carbohydrates consist of long chains of sugar molecules, taking longer to digest and offering sustained energy. They are found in foods such as legumes, vegetables, and whole grains.

Fiber, a type of complex carbohydrate, promotes digestive health by aiding bowel movements and enhancing gut microbiota, which enhance digestion, support vitamin absorption, and provide important signals to the immune system. Fiber also contributes to feelings of fullness.

Generally, complex carbohydrates will support health and weight loss more than simple carbs. However, easily digested, simple carbohydrates can be crucial during the acclimation phases of GLP-1 dosing. For instance, when experiencing nausea or gastrointestinal distress, bland, easily digested carbs such as crackers, toast, or white rice can be soothing and less likely to irritate a sensitive stomach. For individuals with hypoglycemia (low blood sugar), consuming simple carbs can raise blood sugar levels quickly to a safe range. Candy, fruit juice, or glucose tablets are commonly recommended in these instances for their rapid absorption and immediate energy boost, helping alleviate symptoms of confusion, dizziness, or shakiness.

THE BEST SOURCES OF CARBOHYDRATES

- **Whole grains (e.g., quinoa, brown rice, whole-wheat bread, oats):** provide fiber and keep energy stable
- **Starchy vegetables (e.g., sweet potatoes, squash, carrots, beets):** natural sources of fiber and essential vitamins
- **Beans and lentils:** nutrient-dense carbohydrates that also boost protein and fiber intake

FIBER: THE KEY TO DIGESTION, FULLNESS, AND BLOOD SUGAR CONTROL

Fiber supports gut health, digestion, and steady energy levels. It's crucial for preventing constipation, a common GLP-1 side effect. It also slows down digestion, helping you feel full longer and keeping blood sugar stable.

Fiber, a type of carbohydrate that the body cannot digest, is essential for maintaining good health. It comes in two types: soluble and insoluble. Soluble fiber dissolves in water to form a gel-like substance and helps lower blood cholesterol and glucose levels. Insoluble fiber adds bulk to stools and helps prevent constipation.

THE BEST SOURCES OF FIBER

- **Nonstarchy vegetables (e.g., leafy greens, peppers, cucumbers, cruciferous veggies):** low-calorie, high-fiber, and packed with micronutrients
- **Legumes and beans (e.g., chickpeas, black beans, lentils):** dual benefit of protein and fiber
- **Whole grains (e.g., quinoa, farro, oats, brown rice):** provide sustained energy and gut-friendly fiber
- **Fruits (e.g., berries, apples, pears):** naturally sweet with fiber to slow blood sugar spikes
- **Seeds and nuts (e.g., chia, flax, almonds, walnuts):** healthy fats plus fiber for digestive support

FRUITS AND VEGETABLES: ESSENTIAL MICRONUTRIENTS AND COLOR

Although the conversation around weight loss often focuses on macros, micronutrients are just as important. Fruits and vegetables provide vitamins, minerals, antioxidants, and hydration—all essential for energy, digestion, and long-term health.

THE BEST SOURCES OF FRUITS AND VEGETABLES

- **Leafy greens (e.g., spinach, kale, arugula):** high in iron, calcium, and fiber
- **Cruciferous vegetables (e.g., broccoli, cauliflower, brussels sprouts):** packed with antioxidants and fiber
- **Hydrating vegetables (e.g., cucumbers, bell peppers, zucchini):** provide fluids while being easy on digestion
- **Berries and citrus:** high in vitamin C, fiber, and antioxidants
- **Bananas and potatoes:** great sources of potassium to support hydration and muscle function

HEALTHY FATS: FLAVOR AND SATIETY WITHOUT OVERLOAD

Fats help with hormone regulation, brain function, and the absorption of fat-soluble vitamins (A, D, E, and K). They also add flavor and satisfaction to meals. But because fats are calorie-dense, moderation is key—especially when appetite is reduced. Fats provide the densest source of energy among the macronutrients, with each gram of fat providing about 9 calories. Excessive consumption of certain types of fats can lead to excessive calorie intake, weight gain, and health issues. And when you are on a GLP-1 medication, too many high-fat foods can strongly affect GI side effects and low appetite.

THE BEST SOURCES OF HEALTHY FATS

- **Avocados:** heart-healthy monounsaturated fats and fiber
- **Olive oil:** anti-inflammatory and a flavorful alternative to butter
- **Nuts and seeds:** great for snacking, but best in controlled portions
- **Fatty fish (e.g., salmon, sardines, mackerel):** rich in omega-3s for brain and heart health
- **Greek yogurt and cottage cheese:** contain natural fats with high protein

Hydration and Electrolytes: Staying Ahead of Dehydration

Although adequate hydration is important for many health reasons, there is no direct correlation between more hydration and more weight loss. There is some truth to the idea that the habit of drinking more fluids can decrease overall food intake or increase awareness of other healthy habits. But, in a world full of fancy reusable tumblers, folks sometimes drink excessive amounts of fluids. The fact is, our body knows exactly how much water it needs and will expel the excess. With reduced appetites and slowed digestion, though, many people on GLP-1 medications unintentionally drink less water, leading to dehydration and fatigue.

It is important to be more intentional about hydration, but that doesn't mean you need more than the average joe. GLP-1s can decrease the sensation of thirst in the same way they suppress appetite, increasing the risk for dehydration. We also forget how much hydration we get from foods—if we are eating less, we may need to drink a little more.

If you're dealing with side effects, especially vomiting or diarrhea, it is essential to replace these lost fluids to protect your kidneys. But downing yourself in gallons of water per day is unnecessary. As long as you have light-colored urine, you have a moist-feeling mouth, your skin and eyes aren't dry, and you are not fatigued, you're probably drinking enough. Although water is probably the most important beverage for hydration, other options include coffee, diet beverages, herbal teas, sparkling water, unsweetened teas, and any other zero-calorie liquid.

Electrolyte supplements and drinks can be beneficial for folks on GLP-1 medications who are dealing with side effects, very low appetites, and fatigue, or those who engage in high-intensity exercise. Electrolyte drinks can improve hydration levels during and after exercise, especially during prolonged activity or in hot environments. They can help restore electrolyte balance after intense workouts or illnesses (such as vomiting or diarrhea) that lead to imbalances. However, use these products with caution. Many electrolyte drinks contain high levels of sugar that can counteract weight-loss efforts. Regular consumption can lead to too many calories consumed. Excessive intake of electrolytes, such as the amounts found in concentrated supplements, particularly sodium and potassium, can result in imbalances and lead to health issues such as hypertension or heart problems, especially for those with kidney disease.

A Balanced Plate for Weight Loss and Long-Term Health

Eating well on GLP-1 medicines involves more than just choosing the right foods. It's about developing a sustainable eating pattern that fits your lifestyle and supports your health goals. Meal-planning and preparation are also essential components of eating well on GLP-1 medicines. Having a plan helps you make healthier choices and reduces the temptation of convenience foods. Spend some time each week planning your meals, shopping for ingredients, and prepping food in advance.

One of the key principles of eating well on GLP-1 medicines is to focus on balanced meals. Each meal should include a mix of macronutrients—proteins, carbohydrates, and fats. This balance helps ensure that you are getting the energy and nutrients your body needs while also keeping you full and satisfied. I recommend always planning to eat at least three meals per day, even if you're not sure you're hungry. Your job is to try to simply stop when you're full.

Mindful eating is a valuable practice, but sometimes the appetite suppression of these medicines is a little too strong. When you're not hungry, eat the protein first. On the other hand, your experience on your medication may be that you're still pretty hungry. That's normal too! It's important to pay attention to and honor your body's hunger and fullness cues. When you're hungry, eat slowly and savor each bite. Satisfaction comes from more than just the size of the meal—the enjoyment matters too! By being present during your meals, you can enjoy your food more and start to pick up on the subtle signs of satiety to avoid overeating.

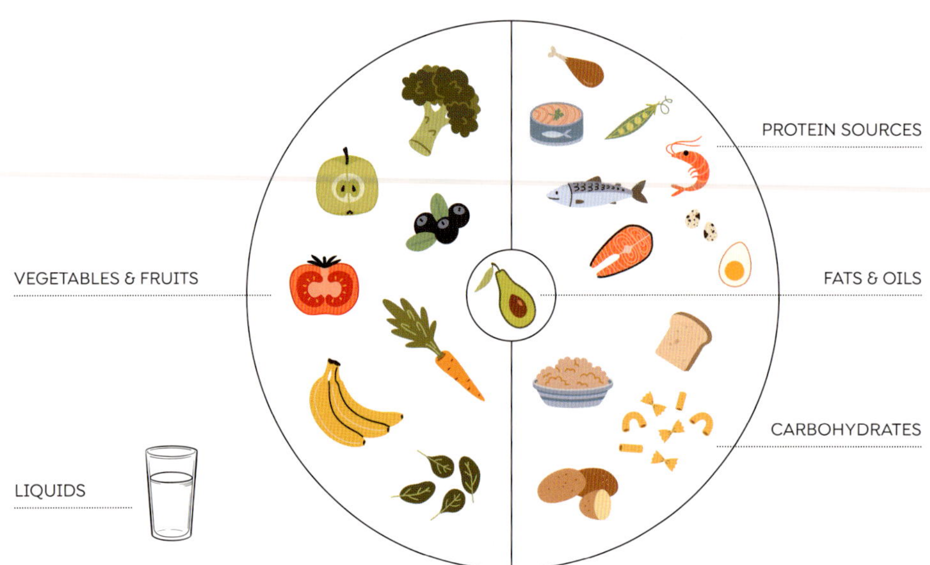

Pro Tips for Getting Your Daily Plan Started

Here are some key tips from a dietitian to remember as you begin your journey.

- Aim for three balanced, filling, and enjoyable meals per day.
- Avoid skipping meals, even if you're not sure you are hungry.
- Prioritize whole foods over processed foods more often than not.
- Limit snacks unless you are physically hungry or losing weight too quickly.
- Remember, the goal is to limit overeating, not under-fuel yourself!
- Target a weight loss of 1 percent per week.
- Prioritize protein. Every meal should include a generous serving of lean protein foods, such as chicken breast, low-fat dairy foods, beans and legumes, seafoods, or meats. Aim for about 30 grams of protein (~5-oz servings) per meal, or more if tolerated.
- Use protein supplements to fill the gaps when your appetite is low.
- Add plenty of fruits and vegetables. To meet your fiber and micronutrient needs, be sure to include produce with every meal, about 1 cup or more. The more variety, the better!
- Always include carbohydrates. GLP-1 medications improve the way your body uses carbohydrates for energy. Include ½ to 1 cup of a fiber-full, starchy food at every meal. Fatigue or GI upset? Increase carbs!
- Hydrate well. Water, coffee, tea, and any other zero-calorie liquids all count. Aim for at least 72 ounces (2.1 L) per day. You probably do not need an electrolyte supplement every day.
- Be mindful of fats and oils. Nuts, cheese, avocados, butter, and oils can be used sparingly (~1-oz [28-g] serving size), with the awareness that these foods can sometimes trigger nausea.

CHAPTER 2

Eating Well on GLP-1 Medicines

Let's face it, GLP-1 medications make eating well and losing weight easier, but that doesn't mean it isn't still hard *sometimes*. Especially when we are first starting our medication (or increasing doses), we can run into some common difficulties. Challenges may also surface when you're approaching maintenance and the appetite suppression you're used to is starting to feel a little less apparent. Then what? Navigating the challenges of eating well on a GLP-1 can be tricky, but thankfully you have this book to help you overcome and thrive!

Empowering yourself and cultivating confidence in your ability to overcome whatever life throws your way are two of the most powerful things you can do when it comes to nutrition. GLP-1 medications may reduce appetite, but they don't replace the need for critical thinking and intentional, mindful eating. Instead of relying on food lists, recipes, recommended portion sizes, or meal schedules, tune in to how your choices about food impact your life. That's where the real growth happens!

Remember, aiming for satiety isn't just about feeling full—it's about feeling nourished, energized, and content after eating. Prioritizing protein, fiber, and balanced meals will help you stay satisfied for longer, but it's just as important to recognize when you've had enough. Knowing what kinds of foods will serve you the best is the cheat code to success on a GLP-1. This awareness is a skill that will serve you well for a lifetime, supporting long-term weight management whether you continue the medication or transition off it. So, instead of waiting for you to go through these struggles, I'd like to share with you some examples of how my patients found success with food!

My patients and I, like so many others, faced common but solvable challenges while adjusting to life on a GLP-1. This cookbook is here to make sure you don't have to struggle through these experiences alone. It offers real-life, practical meals so you can eat well, feel your best, and continue making progress toward your health goals. Whether you're navigating nausea, experiencing food aversions, or just looking for satisfying meals that fit your lifestyle, the recipes here are designed to support you every step of the way.

RACHEL: "I'M ON A GLP-1, BUT MY FAMILY ISN'T—HOW DO I COOK FOR EVERYONE?"

Rachel, a thirty-nine-year-old mom of three, had always been the primary cook in her household. When she started her GLP-1 medication, she quickly realized that her appetite and portion sizes had changed—but her family's hadn't.

"I didn't want to make separate meals for myself, but I also didn't want my husband and kids to feel like they were on a diet just because I was eating differently. I needed meals that worked for all of us."

She decided to find recipes that focus on high-protein, balanced meals with plenty of vegetables and fiber, but are also delicious and satisfying for the whole family. Now, instead of feeling like she's cooking two separate meals, Rachel has family-friendly recipes that support her goals without sacrificing flavor or convenience.

How to Navigate Side Effects

Mild, occasional side effects are normal and should be easily managed with nutrition and over-the-counter products. Most GLP-1 side effects should resolve with time and only feel like a slight inconvenience. However, if your side effects are severe, cause you to miss out on your usual daily activities, or do not improve with these tips, please let your doctor know! Being sick all the time and unable to eat is not how these medications are supposed to work for weight loss!

Managing Digestive Discomfort

When struggling with an upset tummy after taking GLP-1 medications, you should prioritize light, protein-rich, lower-fat recipes that are easy on the stomach. Nausea, constipation, and reflux are some of the most common side effects of GLP-1 medications, but they don't have to derail your progress.

NAUSEA

Many patients who have gone through pregnancy compare the nausea of a GLP-1 with first-trimester morning sickness, including food aversions and sensitivities to smell, with symptoms usually being the worst in the early morning.

Here are some tips that should help:

- Hydrate before you caffeinate.
- Use caution with foods that contain dietary fats.
- Add bland and low-fiber carbs.
- Eat smaller, more frequent meals.
- Avoid skipping meals.
- Drink ice-cold beverages.
- Get some fresh air.
- Try ginger tea, ginger ale, or ginger chews.
- Add a daily B6 vitamin supplement.
- Talk to your doctor about prescribing Zofran.

CARLOS: "I DIDN'T REALIZE I WAS DEHYDRATED UNTIL I FELT AWFUL"

Carlos, a fifty-year-old nurse, was used to drinking coffee all morning and barely sipping water throughout the day. Before starting his GLP-1 medication, he never thought much about hydration. But after a few weeks on the medication, he started experiencing headaches, fatigue, and constipation—and he couldn't figure out why.

"I just felt off, like my body wasn't functioning right. It wasn't until I read about how GLP-1s can increase the risk of dehydration that I realized I needed to be more intentional about drinking fluids."

Carlos found hydrating, electrolyte-rich drink recipes that taste good, such as fruit-infused waters, protein-packed smoothies, and light broths, that helped him stay on top of his hydration without forcing down plain water. He also learned to incorporate high-water foods such as cucumbers, oranges, and zucchini into his meals, making hydration feel effortless.

Now, instead of feeling drained and sluggish, Carlos is more energized, regular, and focused—all because he made hydration a priority in a way that fits his lifestyle.

CONSTIPATION

It is normal for bowel movements to be less frequent while on GLP-1 medication. Remember, these medicines work in part by slowing down your digestive tract, so not going every day is not necessarily a problem! If you feel comfortable and, when you do have a bowel movement, it feels easy to pass and complete, then you probably do not have constipation.

However, if you're bloated, gassy, or having hard stools, these tips can help:

- Aim for about 25 grams of fiber per day, or more as tolerated.
- Add a psyllium husk (Metamucil) fiber supplement.
- Drink plenty of fluids; at least 80 ounces (2.4 L) per day is a great place to start.
- Movement helps! Try short walks or stretching exercises after meals.
- Use a Squatty Potty.
- Talk to your doctor about adding magnesium, MiraLAX, or stool softeners.

REFLUX

Reflux is tricky because many people with obesity experience it long before starting a GLP-1 medication. But, the delayed gastric emptying can certainly exacerbate underlying GERD, especially at night.

Here are some tips to manage your reflux:

- Limit high-fat foods, especially at dinnertime.
- Reduce chocolate, caffeine, alcohol, tobacco, and carbonated beverages.
- Careful with the spice and citrus!
- Stay upright at least 1 hour after eating.
- Take a short walk after meals.
- Try smaller, more frequent meals.
- Try over-the-counter products such as Tums, Pepto-Bismol, or Omeprazole.

Meeting Protein and Fiber Goals without Feeling Overwhelmed

GLP-1s can sometimes reduce appetite so much that eating enough protein and fiber becomes a challenge. But getting enough of both is crucial for weight loss, muscle preservation, and gut health. An easy way to ensure adequate protein throughout the day is to balance your portion sizes across all your meals. Instead of stressing over every gram, it's helpful to estimate! Aim to eat at least 30 grams of protein and 10 grams of fiber with every meal, and try your best to never skip a meal. Keeping these protein foods as lean (low-fat) as possible can help too!

Navigating a Low Appetite and Figuring Out What to Eat When Nothing Sounds Good

Remember, the goal of GLP-1 medication is to keep you full and satisfied between balanced meals—not keep you from ever feeling hungry! If you're losing weight too quickly or not interested in eating at all, I challenge you to try to eat and see what happens. It's normal to think, "I'm not hungry, nothing sounds good, and I don't want to eat" only to sit down to a meal and realize "Oh wow, yeah, this is great. Maybe I was hungry; I can eat this no problem." Being disinterested in eating is different from being unable to eat. For many of us who have struggled with obesity, hunger, and a love of food, it can be hard to know we want to eat if we aren't super excited about it. Not every meal has to be amazing; sometimes it just needs to get the job done.

Here are some tips to help ensure you are eating enough when your appetite is low:

- Check to see if frequent snacking or mindless grazing is preventing you from being able to eat full meals at mealtimes.
- Add a protein shake or supplement to meet your protein goals.
- Choose cooked vegetables over raw. Salads are probably going to be too filling.
- Keep the dietary fats low!
- Plan for simple, neutral-flavored meals that still deliver nutrition.
- Make a soup or smoothie when chewing feels like a chore.
- Talk to your doctor about lowering your medication dose.

MAYA: "I USED TO LOVE COOKING, BUT NOW I GET OVERWHELMED"

Maya, a thirty-two-year-old food lover, had always enjoyed cooking. Trying new recipes, experimenting with flavors, and making meals from scratch had been a source of joy for her. But after starting her GLP-1 medication, she found herself struggling with decision fatigue and feeling overwhelmed in the kitchen.

"I used to spend hours planning meals, but now, with my lower appetite, it's like my brain just shuts down when I think about what to cook. I don't want to eat boring food, but I also don't have the energy to make complicated meals."

She found that simple, balanced recipes with easy-to-follow instructions helped her enjoy cooking again without the stress. She started leaning on one-pan meals, quick-prep proteins, and make-ahead options that still packed bold flavors. Now, instead of feeling lost in the kitchen, she has a go-to plan that keeps meals enjoyable and effortless.

VEGETARIAN AND NON-MEAT OPTIONS FOR WHEN MEAT ISN'T APPEALING

Meat aversion is a common side effect for some people on GLP-1s, but hitting your protein goal is still possible. You can absolutely achieve a healthy, high-protein, muscle-preserving diet while on a GLP-1 and being vegan or vegetarian. (Vegan diets exclude all animal products, whereas vegetarians may choose to eat dairy and eggs.) In fact, a whole food, plant-based–leaning diet has shown incredible health benefits. There are ample sources of protein available for those following a vegan or vegetarian diet, and mindful planning can ensure an adequate intake of all essential amino acids.

Vegan protein sources are diverse and include legumes, such as black beans, chickpeas, kidney beans, and lentils. Nuts and seeds, including almonds, chia seeds, flaxseed, hemp seeds, and walnuts, offer protein and healthy fats. Grains, notably barley, farro, quinoa, and teff, provide not only protein but also various essential nutrients. Soy products such as tofu, tempeh, and edamame are versatile, protein-rich options that can be incorporated into numerous dishes. It is important to ensure you get enough iron, B12, and other nutrients when cutting back on meat, so consider adding a multivitamin if you're finding yourself more vegetarian than carnivore these days.

JAMES: "I USED TO LOVE MEAT, BUT NOW I CAN'T STAND IT"

James, a fifty-five-year-old teacher, had always been a meat-and-potatoes guy. He loved grilling steak, roasting chicken, and making hearty meals. But after starting his GLP-1 medication, he was shocked to find that meat suddenly seemed unappetizing.

"It was the weirdest thing. I'd look at a piece of chicken and feel completely turned off. I didn't know what to eat, and I was worried I wasn't getting enough protein."

James discovered vegetarian and non-meat protein options and started incorporating Greek yogurt bowls, eggs, lentil-based soups, and tofu stir-fries into his diet. Having flavorful, high-protein alternatives made it easier for him to enjoy his meals again without forcing himself to eat foods that no longer appealed to him.

Overcoming Fatigue

A poor appetite and apathy toward food usually manifest as fatigue. Remember, the GLP-1 medications are supposed to help you use the nutrients you consume as energy more efficiently, not less. If you're feeling run-down, tired all the time, in need of extra naps, unable to exercise, or like you're oversleeping since starting your medication, you're most likely not eating enough! Sometimes chronic undereating can lead to low blood sugar, causing dizziness, weakness, or lack of focus. Adding a few small carb-based snacks throughout the day can help you maintain steady blood sugar levels, keeping you energized. It's also normal to need more calories if you've increased your exercise intensity, duration, or frequency. Remember, fueling is important for the enjoyability of your workouts and recovery!

Here are some tips for overcoming fatigue:

- Monitor your rate of weight loss. Eat enough to lose weight at a slow and steady pace. Target 2 to 3 pounds (0.9 to 1.4 kg) per week, not more!
- Never skip meals.
- Have breakfast first thing in the morning if you can.
- Consider your schedule and look for places to add snacks between meals.
- Add more carbohydrates, especially the easily digestible ones.
- Hydrate well. Electrolytes may really help here.

MARK: "I KEEP FORGETTING TO EAT UNTIL IT'S TOO LATE"

Mark, a fifty-two-year-old IT specialist, had always been an "eat when I'm hungry" kind of guy. But once he started his GLP-1 medication, his hunger cues became so subtle that he often went hours—sometimes the entire day—without eating, only to realize he was suddenly exhausted, weak, and lightheaded.

"I never really felt hungry, so I'd just keep working, assuming my body didn't need food. Then I'd hit a wall, feeling totally drained and scrambling to eat whatever was easiest—usually not the healthiest choice."

Mark eventually figured out how to build a structure that worked for his new appetite. He found quick protein-packed snacks he could eat even when he wasn't particularly hungry, such as Greek yogurt with nuts, protein smoothies, and cottage cheese with fruit. He also started meal prepping easy-to-reheat lunches so he didn't have to make decisions when he was too busy.

With these small changes, Mark stopped skipping meals, had more steady energy throughout the day, and felt in control of his eating habits again—without having to rely on hunger signals that weren't showing up like they used to.

Your New Perception of Hunger and Fullness

It's not unusual for people who have struggled with obesity to have an unhelpful or complicated relationship with the concepts of hunger and fullness. Many of us only ever knew it as opposite sides of a coin: starving or stuffed. And many of us have been team #cleanplateclub since childhood! But once on GLP-1 medications, we may no longer ever feel "starving," so it's a little hard to know if you're hungry.

I typically recommend planning for three scheduled, predictable, balanced meals a day, regardless of your perception of hunger—especially in the beginning of your journey. If you feel hungry on a GLP-1, you probably are. And you should eat! I know it can be hard to trust your perception of appetite, especially if it was so unreliable or failed you for years. But hunger isn't a bad thing. It's a good thing to have a healthy appetite while on a GLP-1 medication so you can eat nutritiously and meet your protein goals.

If you're truly constantly hungry, you probably need to eat more food, and maybe different foods or on a different daily schedule. But remember, hunger is not the same as food noise (see page 27). Hunger isn't just about an empty stomach or energy balance; it's a whole-body experience influenced by biology.

SAMANTHA: "I THOUGHT I WAS EATING HEALTHY, BUT I WAS ALWAYS HUNGRY"

Samantha, a thirty-eight-year-old mom of two, had been on her GLP-1 medication for a few months and was thrilled with her progress. But she started noticing a pattern: she would eat a small salad or some fruit for lunch, thinking she was making a healthy choice, only to find herself ravenous a few hours later.

"I was eating way less than before, but I wasn't feeling full. I'd end up snacking on random things, and sometimes I'd even feel a little shaky. It was frustrating because I was trying to do the right thing, but I didn't feel satisfied."

Samantha realized she needed to prioritize protein, fiber, and healthy fats to feel full longer. She started adding grilled chicken or cottage cheese to her salads, pairing her fruit with Greek yogurt, and incorporating whole grains such as quinoa and farro into her meals. The difference was immediate. She felt fuller for longer, had more energy, and stopped reaching for snacks out of desperation.

Here are some common sensations associated with hunger that may be a signal that you need to eat soon.

- **Stomach growling:** Your stomach makes noise as it contracts and releases digestive juices in anticipation of food.
- **Empty or hollow sensation:** This is a mild discomfort in the stomach that grows stronger if you don't eat.
- **Low energy and fatigue:** Your body slows down when it runs low on fuel, making you feel tired or sluggish.
- **Difficulty concentrating:** Hunger can make it harder to focus, because your brain prefers glucose (sugar) as its main energy source.
- **Irritability ("hangry" feeling):** Blood sugar levels drop when you haven't eaten, which can affect mood and make you feel more impatient or cranky.

Navigating Cravings and Food Noise

Food noise is a term used to describe persistent thoughts about food that are not necessarily driven by physical hunger. It's when food is constantly on your mind—whether you're planning your next meal, craving something specific, or feeling a compulsion to eat even when you're not physically hungry. To be clear, everyone has occasional cravings or preferences and enjoys highly palatable food from time to time, eating beyond physical fullness. A craving is easily satisfied and often brings joy! Food noise, though, is difficult to suppress and is often so intrusive that it causes distress. Food noise often makes us feel out of control, guilty, shameful, or incapable.

Several factors can increase our perception of hunger, cravings, and food noise, whether due to biological, psychological, or environmental influences. And although your GLP-1 medication may make it easier to tolerate hunger and food noise, it may not always control them as well as we'd hoped.

If you're really struggling despite being on a GLP-1 medication, consider checking in on some of these nonfood factors.

- **Poor sleep:** Lack of sleep throws hunger hormones out of balance. Research shows that sleep deprivation increases ghrelin (hunger) and decreases leptin (fullness), making you more likely to overeat. It can also increase cravings for high-calorie foods.
- **Stress and cortisol:** When you're stressed, your body releases cortisol, which can increase appetite. This is a survival mechanism—your body is preparing for a "fight or flight" response, even if the stress isn't physical.
- **Highly processed foods:** Foods high in refined carbohydrates and low in fiber and protein digest quickly, leading to a cycle of hunger and overeating. Many foods are designed to be hyper-palatable, meaning they trigger a dopamine release, enticing you to consume more than your body may actually need.

KEY DIFFERENCES BETWEEN HUNGER AND FOOD NOISE		
	HUNGER	**FOOD NOISE**
What is the cause?	Biological need for energy	Psychological cravings, habits, emotions, biological dysfunction
What hormones are involved?	Ghrelin (hunger), leptin (fullness)	Dopamine (reward), cortisol (stress)
How does it feel?	Empty stomach, stomach growling, low energy	Constant thoughts about food, cravings, impulse to eat
How does it develop?	Gradually over time or after increased energy expenditure	Can appear suddenly, even after just eating
What satisfies it?	Any nutritious food that offers satiety after eating	Often specific foods, especially highly processed or "comfort" foods
Does it go away after eating?	Yes, when properly nourished	No, it may persist even when physically full

- **Eating too quickly or while distracted:** Your brain needs about twenty minutes to register fullness. If you eat too quickly or without awareness of your intake, you may consume more food before your body realizes it's satisfied.
- **Low-protein or low-fiber diet:** Protein and fiber slow digestion and keep you full longer. Diets low in these nutrients can lead to frequent hunger.
- **Inadequate hydration:** Low fluid balance can result in fatigue, which we can perceive as hunger.
- **Extreme dieting and calorie restriction:** Cutting calories too aggressively can increase hunger, so please, don't skip meals. Include all food groups. Be sure to eat enough!
- **Environmental triggers:** Food-related habits are hard to break. You may still find yourself feeling out of control sometimes around specific foods or situations.

DAVID: "SOCIAL EVENTS STRESS ME OUT—WHAT DO I EAT?"

David, a forty-six-year-old extrovert, used to love going out to dinner with friends, celebrating birthdays, and hosting game nights with plenty of food. But after starting his GLP-1 medication, he found himself anxious about social situations where food was the focus.

"Before, I'd just eat what was served and enjoy myself. Now, I get full so quickly that I worry people will notice or ask why I'm not eating much. I don't want to be the guy explaining my medication at every meal."

David eventually learned how to choose high-protein, fiber-rich options when eating out, navigate small portion sizes without feeling awkward, and bring a dish to share that works for him but also pleases a crowd. With these strategies, he's been able to enjoy social events without stress, stay on track with his goals, and keep food from being a source of anxiety.

Overcoming a Weight-Loss Plateau

Before we dive into why we plateau and how to manage it, let's first be really honest with ourselves. Are we actually consistent with our plan? Of course, no one expects perfection, but if you've been losing steadily and then, well, not, we need to understand if there is a clear reason before we make any big changes to the plan that was working! Sometimes overcoming a plateau just means correcting back to what works. So, the first step is to do some self-assessment: Are you continuing to eat in the way that was producing weight loss before? Are you hitting protein goals, monitoring your portion sizes, and getting your fiber and veggies? Or has something fallen off? Sometimes it's not a plateau; it's just an explainable maintenance phase because we've been living and eating like a person in maintenance. Holiday, vacation, a stressful week at work, or kids home sick? No biggie. Pick up where you left off and your weight loss should too!

A weight-loss plateau is a short period of time—about two to four weeks long—during which your weight remains the same despite continuing your usual healthy eating and exercise habits. It can feel discouraging, but it's a completely normal part of the weight-loss process. It's actually not normal to lose weight every week during a weight-loss journey. It's also normal for weight loss to slow down as you get closer to your goals. The last 10 pounds (5 kg) should take twice as long (or longer!) to lose as the first 10! If you are averaging 0.5 to 1 percent body weight loss per week over the course of a month, you're doing just fine!

For example, a 200-pound (91-kg) person should expect to lose 1 to 2 pounds (0.5 to 0.9 kg) per week on average while on a GLP-1. When they get to 160 pounds (73 kg), their new expectation is a little less—0.8 to 1.6 pounds (0.4 to 0.7 kg) per week.

There are several reasons your weight might plateau or stall. When it does, you're not doing something wrong. Here are some common causes and potential solutions to help you navigate a plateau along your GLP-1 journey.

YOUR BODY ADAPTS TO CHANGES

When you first start losing weight, your body responds quickly to changes in diet and exercise. Especially if you've made big changes! However, as you settle into your new habits, your body sees this as your new normal. This means that as you get lighter, you may need to adjust your habits (layer in more healthy changes), reduce your calorie intake, or increase the impact of your exercise routine to continue making progress.

Try reassessing your calories and macronutrients:

- Recalculate your daily calorie needs. As you lose weight, your calorie needs decrease. Try using an online calculator to adjust your intake based on your new weight.
- Track your food intake (even if just for a short time). Use an app or food journal to make sure you're eating what you think you are. It's easy to underestimate portion sizes or forget about snacks.
- Check your macronutrient balance. Consider increasing your protein and fiber goals to help with satiety (feeling fuller longer).

EXERCISE AND CHANGES IN MUSCLE MASS

Adding in exercise is incredibly health promoting for a bunch of reasons that have nothing to do with weight loss. It's not uncommon, though, for a new exercise routine to actually slow down the rate with which you lose weight. This is normal! Sometimes more exercise means more appetite, so it's important to be aware of how, if any, your food intake increases. And when strength training, you may be losing fat but gaining muscle (this is great!), which could explain why the scale isn't moving as much even though your body composition is improving.

Try switching up your workout routine:

- Increase exercise intensity or duration. If you're doing only steady-state cardio (such as walking), try adding distance, weight, or some interval training (run/walk).
- Strength train regularly. If you're not already, add two or three days of strength training per week to build lean muscle, which helps boost your metabolism in the long term.
- Change your exercise mode. Mix things up! If you've been walking, try cycling or swimming. Different exercises can activate different muscle groups and prevent your body from adapting.
- Take a break. It might be time for a rest day (or more) or a "deload" week. Rest and recovery is important for weight loss—maybe even more than "calories burned."

PSYCHOLOGICAL AND EMOTIONAL FACTORS

Stress, lack of sleep, and emotional eating can all affect your progress. These factors can impact your hormones, appetite, and ability to make healthy choices, which may cause a temporary stall in weight loss. Try optimizing sleep and stress management:

- Aim for seven to nine hours of sleep. Sleep is crucial for hormone balance, appetite, and recovery. Try to set a consistent bedtime routine and wake-up time to help regulate your sleep cycle. Explore ways to improve your sleeping environment. Maybe you need some black-out curtains, a sound machine, new sheets, or a better pillow?
- Practice stress-relief techniques. Chronic stress can hinder weight loss. Add in relaxing activities that bring you peace and joy, such as yoga, meditation, deep breathing, or even a short walk outside, to reduce stress levels.
- Engage your health care team for support. Talk to your doctor about counseling, supplements, hormones, and medications if insomnia, anxiety, or depression are struggles.
- Identify emotional eating triggers. Are there situations or emotions that lead you to overeat? Try journaling your feelings before you eat to identify patterns and find healthier coping mechanisms.
- Practice mindful eating. Slow down and savor each bite, sit at a table, and limit distractions. Eating mindfully can help you recognize when you're full, reducing overeating.

IT'S TIME FOR A GLP-1 DOSE TITRATION

Feeling more food noise? Less satiety after meals? Notice that your portion sizes are creeping larger? It may just be time to titrate up your GLP-1 dose! This is an expected part of the journey. Remember, in the clinical trials, the lower doses are described as "loading" or "starter" doses, while the higher doses are "therapeutic." There's no shame in moving on up to achieve your goals!

As you consider your weight-loss plateau and why it might be happening, don't forget to ask yourself a very important question: Do I actually need or want to keep losing weight, or could this be maintenance? When weight loss feels frustrating, it's important to shift your mindset, focus on your non-scale victories, and evaluate your goals:

- Track your measurements. Use a tape measure to check your waist circumference. Losing belly fat, but staying the same on the scale, means you're doing all the right things. Sometimes the scale doesn't reflect changes in body composition (fat loss and muscle gain).
- Notice how your clothes fit. Are your jeans feeling looser? Are you wearing smaller sizes? These are signs of progress.
- Celebrate energy and mood. Are you feeling more energetic, sleeping better, or feeling more confident? These are all important signs that your lifestyle changes are improving your health and quality of life. The scale isn't everything!
- Set small, achievable goals: Break your big weight-loss goal into smaller, manageable milestones. Celebrate each success along the way.
- Focus on sustainability: Aim for lifestyle changes that you can maintain in the long run, not just quick fixes. Consistency is key to lasting results.

Plateaus and stalls can be challenging, but they're not permanent. With a little tweaking, patience, and self-compassion, you can get back on track. Trust the process, celebrate your successes, and keep focusing on building a healthy lifestyle—both for today and for the long term. Remember: progress is progress, no matter how slow. You're doing amazing, and every step you take brings you closer to your goals!

Meal-Planning for GLP-1 Success

Meal-planning is a cornerstone of success when it comes to eating well on GLP-1 medicines. By taking the time to plan and prepare your meals, you can ensure that you have nutritious options available and reduce the likelihood of making choices in the moment that don't align with your goals. Start by setting aside some time each week to plan your meals. Consider your schedule, your dietary preferences, and your nutritional needs. Make a list of the meals you want to prepare and the ingredients you'll need. This can help you stay organized and make your grocery shopping more efficient.

Aim for variety, and an assortment of proteins, vegetables, and whole grains to keep your meals interesting and nutritionally balanced. Look for recipes—like those in this book—that are simple to prepare and can be made in batches, so you have leftovers for busy days. Preparation is key. Spend some time each week prepping ingredients and cooking meals in advance. This can include chopping vegetables, cooking grains, and portioning out snacks. Having ready-to-eat meals and snacks on hand can make it easier to avoid unhealthy choices.

To get you started, I've curated some meal plans for you with recipes from this book.

5 WELL-BALANCED DAYS

Eating well doesn't have to mean sacrificing flavor or fun! Most days on your GLP-1 journey should follow a balanced approach, where all foods can fit but you prioritize your proteins, whole foods, and fiber. Here are five potential well-balanced days of meals.

DAY 1					
RECIPE	CALORIES	FAT (G)	PROTEIN (G)	CARB (G)	DIETARY FIBER (G)
Refried Bean Quesadillas	350	5	27	49	1
Pizza Chickpeas	230	5	13	36	12
Loaf Pan Shawarma Chicken	340	5	30	44	4
Healthier Drive-Thru Egg Muffin Sandwiches	360	12	32	32	3
Side of fruit with your sandwich	85	0	1	20	2
TOTAL	**1,365**	**27**	**103**	**181**	**22**

DAY 2					
RECIPE	CALORIES	FAT (G)	PROTEIN (G)	CARB (G)	DIETARY FIBER (G)
Cozy Autumn Roasted Salad	440	15	32	45	11
2 servings of Buffalo Chicken Dip	140	2	22	6	0
1 cup veggies with your dip	70	0	1	20	2
Breaded Chicken Tenders with Tzatziki	290	5	39	25	3
No-Egg Savory Breakfast Bowls	340	12	44	13	1
TOTAL	**1,280**	**34**	**138**	**109**	**17**

DAY 3					
RECIPE	CALORIES	FAT (G)	PROTEIN (G)	CARB (G)	DIETARY FIBER (G)
Asian Tuna Salad	210	7	28	10	4
Creamy Grape Salad	270	12	7	36	2
Slow Cooker Cuban Pork Tenderloin	190	5	32	3	0
1905 Salad	260	18	15	10	2
Warm Apple Cinnamon Oatmeal	400	4	34	65	7
TOTAL	1,330	46	116	124	15

DAY 4					
RECIPE	CALORIES	FAT (G)	PROTEIN (G)	CARB (G)	DIETARY FIBER (G)
BBQ Chicken Flatbreads	420	10	48	35	5
Mocktail Margarita	25	0	0	8	0
Broccoli Chicken Alfredo	420	8	43	52	8
Cannoli Bowl	370	15	41	19	1
TOTAL	1,235	33	132	114	14

DAY 5					
RECIPE	CALORIES	FAT (G)	PROTEIN (G)	CARB (G)	DIETARY FIBER (G)
Thai Peanut Chicken Salad	400	21	41	16	5
Nonalcoholic Shandy	60	0	0	14	0
Air-Fryer Tofu with Cucumber Celery Salad	330	19	23	18	4
Western Omelet	340	18	37	7	0
Serve omelet with side of fruit	85	0	1	20	2
TOTAL	1,215	58	102	75	11

5 LOW-APPETITE DAYS

On days when your appetite is particularly low, consider softer and liquid foods for easier digestion. Keeping fats and fiber lower on these days can also help you feel capable of meeting your calorie and protein needs without feeling too full. Here are five days of options.

DAY 1					
RECIPE	CALORIES	FAT (G)	PROTEIN (G)	CARB (G)	DIETARY FIBER (G)
Instant Pot Steel-Cut Oats	270	3	21	45	5
Tomato Lentil Soup	230	2	19	35	6
Greek Yogurt Rolls	200	3	11	33	1
Shrimp Pasta in Fresh Herb Sauce	390	10	35	44	6
Basic Freezer Smoothie	200	1	27	24	4
TOTAL	1,290	19	113	181	22

DAY 2					
RECIPE	**CALORIES**	**FAT (G)**	**PROTEIN (G)**	**CARB (G)**	**DIETARY FIBER (G)**
Pepperoni Chaffles	240	7	27	18	1
Potato Leek Soup with Turkey Bacon	300	6	21	44	4
2 servings of Simple Poached Chicken	280	6	52	0	0
1 cup white rice with your chicken	205	1	4	45	1
1 cup steamed veggies with your chicken	80	1	1	15	2
Deviled Eggs	180	11	15	3	0
TOTAL	**1,285**	**32**	**120**	**125**	**8**

DAY 3					
RECIPE	**CALORIES**	**FAT (G)**	**PROTEIN (G)**	**CARB (G)**	**DIETARY FIBER (G)**
PB&J Yogurt Parfait	280	7	31	24	8
Salmon Bagel Cucumber Salad	220	5	29	18	2
Slow Cooker Garlic Rosemary Chicken	330	4	33	40	5
1 cup white rice with your chicken	205	1	4	45	1
1 cup steamed veggies with your chicken	80	1	1	15	2
Banana Churro Smoothie	280	5	19	45	4
TOTAL	**1,395**	**23**	**117**	**187**	**22**

DAY 4					
RECIPE	**CALORIES**	**FAT (G)**	**PROTEIN (G)**	**CARB (G)**	**DIETARY FIBER (G)**
Florentine Omelet	290	15	33	7	1
Loaded Miso Soup	450	8	37	58	6
Butternut Squash Pasta Bake	470	7	33	74	12
Mango Lassi	200	1	24	26	1
TOTAL	**1,410**	**31**	**127**	**165**	**20**

DAY 5					
RECIPE	**CALORIES**	**FAT (G)**	**PROTEIN (G)**	**CARB (G)**	**DIETARY FIBER (G)**
Cheesy Grits with Collards and Canadian Bacon	340	2	31	49	2
Egg Roll Bowl	300	4	32	37	4
White Chicken Chili	330	9	31	32	7
Cold Brew Kefir Smoothie	400	10	20	68	6
TOTAL	**1,370**	**25**	**114**	**186**	**19**

5 HUNGRY DAYS

On days when you feel hungrier, don't panic! Remember that you should feel like you have an appetite most of the time. In fact, you're human. Increases in stress, activity, or simply the recent days of calorie deficits can make you feel more hungry than usual, and that's okay! Listening to your body and feeding it high-quality, balanced meals are skills that will serve you well for the rest of your life.

DAY 1					
RECIPE	**CALORIES**	**FAT (G)**	**PROTEIN (G)**	**CARB (G)**	**DIETARY FIBER (G)**
Curried Breakfast Egg Salad Wrap	530	26	26	52	3
Brothy Beans and Sausage	480	15	41	49	11
Grilled Flank Steak with Chimichurri Rice	470	18	43	34	5
Serve with 1 cup steamed vegetable	80	1	1	15	2
Peanut Butter and Raspberry Rice Cakes	190	2	12	30	7
TOTAL	**1,750**	**62**	**123**	**180**	**28**

DAY 2					
RECIPE	**CALORIES**	**FAT (G)**	**PROTEIN (G)**	**CARB (G)**	**DIETARY FIBER (G)**
Savory Overnight Oats	410	5	53	45	5
Jamaican Jerk Beef Patty Skillet	430	10	36	46	4
Serve with 1 cup white rice	205	1	4	45	1
Serve with 1 cup steamed vegetable	80	1	1	15	2
Sheet Pan BBQ Pork Tenderloin	360	4	39	42	5
Serve with 1 cup steamed vegetable	80	1	1	15	2
Cauliflower Hummus and raw vegetables	130	7	5	15	4
TOTAL	**1,695**	**29**	**139**	**223**	**23**

DAY 3					
RECIPE	**CALORIES**	**FAT (G)**	**PROTEIN (G)**	**CARB (G)**	**DIETARY FIBER (G)**
Turkey "Sausage" Hash	490	11	38	67	6
Sandwich Shop Chopped Salad	400	24	29	20	5
Smash Burgers with Air-Fried Potato Wedges	500	12	33	67	4
Burger Sauce	20	0	2	3	0
Chocolate Peanut Butter Chia Pudding	250	8	12	36	8
TOTAL	**1,660**	**55**	**114**	**193**	**23**

DAY 4					
RECIPE	**CALORIES**	**FAT (G)**	**PROTEIN (G)**	**CARB (G)**	**DIETARY FIBER (G)**
Protein Pancakes	530	11	29	78	3
Serve pancakes with a side of fruit	85	0	1	20	2
Taco Bowl	560	17	37	62	11
Rotisserie Chicken Caesar Kale Salad	420	23	40	16	1
Protein Tiramisu	250	5	8	42	2
TOTAL	**1,845**	**56**	**115**	**218**	**19**

DAY 5					
RECIPE	**CALORIES**	**FAT (G)**	**PROTEIN (G)**	**CARB (G)**	**DIETARY FIBER (G)**
Cannoli Bowl	370	15	41	19	1
Veggie Salad Wrap	430	18	30	55	18
Nonalcoholic Shandy	60	0	0	14	0
Steak Fajitas with Air-Fried Plantains	630	17	35	93	8
TOTAL	**1,490**	**50**	**106**	**181**	**27**

TIMING NOTE

Each chapter includes a time estimate in the chapter title (30 minutes for breakfasts, 50 minutes for dinners, etc.). The recipes in that chapter take that amount of time—or less! Note that the times include active cooking, but not extra time for marinating, chilling, slow cooking, or the like. Check the timing section below the recipe to plan ahead on your timing.

CHAPTER 3

18 Breakfasts in 30 Minutes

A balanced breakfast sets the tone for the day, providing you with the energy and nutrients you need to start your morning on a positive note. It's normal to feel "not so hungry" in the morning when you are on a GLP-1 medication, but skipping breakfast often backfires. Remember: eating enough on purpose can prevent overeating by accident! And if you're still struggling with nighttime cravings, carbs at breakfast might help! In this chapter, you'll find a variety of breakfast recipes that are easy to prepare and packed with wholesome ingredients. Whether it's a savory egg dish or a sweet bowl of oats, there's something here for everyone.

CURRIED BREAKFAST EGG SALAD WRAP

YIELD:
1 SERVING

PREP TIME:
5 MINUTES

Although you might think of curry as more of a lunchtime flavor, it really shines at breakfast, too. In addition to tasting great, the turmeric found in many curry powder blends has been shown to have anti-inflammatory properties.

---

2 eggs, hard-boiled and chopped
2 tablespoons (30 g) plain nonfat Greek yogurt
1 tablespoon (14 g) light mayonnaise
1 teaspoon (2 g) curry powder
1 teaspoon (2 g) chopped cilantro
¼ teaspoon salt
⅛ teaspoon ground black pepper
1 high-protein wrap (at least 9 g of protein per wrap)

In a small bowl, stir eggs, yogurt, mayonnaise, curry powder, cilantro, salt, and pepper. Lay wrap on a flat surface, pile egg salad on top, and roll up, folding the edges in like a burrito.

VEGETARIAN

NUTRITIONAL ANALYSIS

SERVING SIZE: 1 wrap (260 g)

PER SERVING: 530 calories; 26 g fat; 26 g protein; 52 g carbohydrate; 3 g dietary fiber

INSTANT POT STEEL-CUT OATS

Steel-cut oats offer a different texture than your run-of-the-mill oatmeal, and texture can be key to enjoying this amazing ingredient! Oats can take a long time to cook on the stovetop, but using an Instant Pot speeds things up considerably. Plus there's no stirring: just dump the ingredients in and set it. Add a couple of hard-boiled eggs to this meal to meet your protein targets.

YIELD: 6 SERVINGS

PREP TIME: 5 MINUTES

COOK TIME: 15 MINUTES, PLUS COOLING TIME

---

1 cup (160 g) steel-cut oats
2 cups (473 ml) nonfat milk
1 cup (237 ml) water
2 tablespoons (30 ml) honey
1 teaspoon (3 g) ground cinnamon
½ teaspoon salt

FOR SERVING

1 cup (235 g) plain nonfat Greek yogurt
1 cup (237 ml) high-protein cereal (at least 12 g protein per serving)
1 cup (237 ml) fresh or frozen fruit of your choice

In an Instant Pot, stir steel-cut oats, milk, water, honey, cinnamon, and salt. Cook on manual (high) for 4 minutes. Let pressure release naturally. Stir and let cool for 10 minutes. The oatmeal will thicken as it cools.

To serve: Top with yogurt, cereal, and fruit.

GLUTEN FREE: Use GF oats

VEGETARIAN

NUTRITIONAL ANALYSIS

SERVING SIZE: 1 cup (227 g)

PER SERVING: 270 calories; 3 g fat; 21 g protein; 45 g carbohydrate; 5 g dietary fiber

PEPPERONI CHAFFLES

YIELD:
2 SERVINGS

PREP TIME:
5 MINUTES

COOK TIME:
15 MINUTES

What the heck are chaffles, you ask? Easy: they were originally "cheese waffles," but chaffle *is kind of fun to say, right? If you don't have a waffle maker, these can be cooked like pancakes in a skillet sprayed with cooking spray. But* chancakes *is less fun to say.*

---

2 large eggs
2 large egg whites
¾ cup (122 g) nonfat cottage cheese
¼ cup (28 g) shredded fat-free mozzarella cheese
¼ cup (31 g) all-purpose flour
1 teaspoon (3 g) Italian seasoning
16 slices (30 g) turkey pepperoni, chopped

In a medium bowl, whisk eggs, egg whites, cottage cheese, mozzarella, flour, and Italian seasoning. For a creamier consistency, use a blender to blend ingredients until smooth. Stir in pepperoni.

Heat a mini waffle maker according to the manufacturer's instructions. Spray liberally with cooking spray. Scoop ¼ cup (60 ml) batter into the waffle maker and cook 2 to 3 minutes, until golden brown. Repeat with remaining batter.

NUTRITIONAL ANALYSIS

SERVING SIZE: 4 mini waffles (183 g)

PER SERVING: 240 calories; 7 g fat; 27 g protein; 18 g carbohydrate; 1 g dietary fiber

NO-EGG SAVORY BREAKFAST BOWLS

YIELD: 4 SERVINGS

PREP TIME: 10 MINUTES

COOK TIME: 15 MINUTES

Need a break from eggs for breakfast? Try this easy meal prep-friendly bowl. If you're not familiar with kimchi, it's a fermented cabbage dish that originated in Korea. It's crunchy, a little spicy, and so good for your gut! You can find it in most supermarkets in the natural foods section or in the refrigerated section near the tofu. Fermented sauerkraut is a good substitution.

---

1 pound (454 g) ground chicken
½ teaspoon salt
¼ teaspoon ground black pepper
1 medium zucchini, chopped
1 medium onion, chopped
1 teaspoon (5 g) garlic powder
1 container (16 ounces, or 454 g) nonfat cottage cheese
½ cup (75 g) kimchi

Heat a large skillet over medium heat and spray with cooking spray. Add ground chicken, salt, and pepper. Cook 7 to 8 minutes, until no longer pink. Add zucchini, onion, and garlic powder, and cook 7 to 8 minutes, until softened. Scoop ¼ of the cottage cheese into a bowl or meal prep container. Top with chicken mixture and a couple tablespoons of kimchi.

GLUTEN FREE

NUTRITIONAL ANALYSIS

SERVING SIZE: 1 cup (333 g)

PER SERVING: 340 calories; 12 g fat; 44 g protein; 13 g carbohydrate; 1 g dietary fiber

HEALTHIER DRIVE-THRU EGG MUFFIN SANDWICHES

YIELD: 6 SERVINGS

PREP TIME: 15 MINUTES

COOK TIME: 15 MINUTES

Now, we know that there is no spinach or tomato in the fast-food version of this easy breakfast, but adding veggies to a meal is the best way to increase the nutrients! This is also a great way to use up any leftover veggies that might be floating around in your fridge: Roasted broccoli? Cooked onions and peppers? One lone zucchini? Toss 'em in!

---

12 large eggs

2 teaspoons (12 g) salt

1 teaspoon (3 g) ground black pepper

2 cups (160 g) baby spinach, chopped

1 cup (244 g) cherry tomatoes, halved

6 high-protein English muffins (5–8 g protein each), split and toasted

6 slices breakfast ham

6 slices fat-free Cheddar cheese

Preheat oven to 350°F (180°C, or gas mark 4). Generously spray a 12-cup muffin pan with cooking spray.

In a large bowl, whisk eggs, salt, and pepper until fully combined. Stir in spinach and tomatoes.

Pour egg mixture into the prepared muffin pan, dividing the mixture evenly between the cups. Bake 15 to 20 minutes, until eggs are set. Remove from oven and cool slightly.

To assemble: Lay English muffin bottoms on a flat surface. Layer on one slice of ham, one slice of cheese, and two egg cups. Top with English muffin tops, and wrap each individually in plastic wrap or parchment paper. Freeze until ready to serve.

To reheat, remove from plastic wrap or paper. Wrap in a paper towel, and defrost in the microwave for 3 minutes. Then microwave on high for 1 to 2 minutes, until warmed through.

NUTRITIONAL ANALYSIS

SERVING SIZE: 1 sandwich (253 g)

PER SERVING: 360 calories; 12 g fat; 32 g protein; 32 g carbohydrate; 3 g dietary fiber

DINER BREAKFAST

When you want to have the diner experience without the sticky booth seats, this recipe is here for you. Don't forget the coffee! This would also be great as a solo breakfast-for-dinner option.

YIELD:
1 SERVING

PREP TIME:
10 MINUTES

COOK TIME:
15 MINUTES

---

1 medium potato, peeled and shredded
¼ cup (29 g) diced onion
¼ cup (65 g) chickpeas
½ teaspoon salt
¼ teaspoon ground black pepper
2 eggs
2 slices turkey bacon
Hot sauce for serving (optional)

Heat a large skillet over medium heat and spray with cooking spray. Cook potato, onion, chickpeas, salt, and pepper 5 to 8 minutes, until onions are softened and potatoes are crisp. Remove potato hash to a plate and cover to keep warm. In the same skillet, cook turkey bacon and eggs until bacon is crispy and eggs are cooked to your liking. Serve with hot sauce, if desired.

NUTRITIONAL ANALYSIS

SERVING SIZE: 1 breakfast plate (340 g)

PER SERVING: 340 calories; 16 g fat; 32 g protein; 45 g carbohydrate; 6 g dietary fiber

STRAWBERRY VANILLA OVERNIGHT OATS

YIELD: 1 SERVING

PREP TIME: 5 MINUTES

Substitutions are key to not getting bored with your breakfasts. For this dish, use blueberries, blackberries, grapes, apples, mango . . . really, almost any fruit will work. Another timesaving trick is to buy frozen bagged fruit that is already peeled and prepped and add it to your jar before refrigerating. The fruit will defrost overnight and be ready to stir into your oatmeal.

- **½ cup (40 g) old-fashioned rolled oats**
- **½ cup (118 ml) nonfat milk**
- **½ cup (118 g) plain nonfat Greek yogurt**
- **1 scoop vanilla protein powder**
- **2 teaspoons (5 g) chia seeds**
- **½ teaspoon ground cinnamon**
- **½ cup (140 g) fresh strawberries, diced**

In a jar or bowl with a lid, stir oats, milk, yogurt, protein powder, chia seeds, and cinnamon. Cover and refrigerate 8 hours, or overnight. Before serving, top with strawberries.

GLUTEN FREE: Use GF oats

VEGETARIAN

NUTRITIONAL ANALYSIS

SERVING SIZE: 1½ cups (367 g)

PER SERVING: 360 calories; 6 g fat; 32 g protein; 52 g carbohydrate; 9 g dietary fiber

SAVORY OVERNIGHT OATS

YIELD: 1 SERVING

PREP TIME: 10 MINUTES

Don't like a sweet breakfast? Who says that oats can't be savory!

- **½ cup (40 g) old-fashioned rolled oats**
- **½ cup (118 ml) nonfat milk**
- **½ cup (118 g) plain nonfat Greek yogurt**
- **1 scoop unflavored protein powder**
- **1 scallion, chopped**
- **1 tablespoon (15 g) dry-packed sun-dried tomatoes, chopped**
- **1 slice Canadian bacon, chopped**
- **1 teaspoon (4 g) everything bagel seasoning**

In a jar or bowl with a lid, stir oats, milk, yogurt, protein powder, scallion, sun-dried tomatoes, bacon, and everything bagel seasoning. Cover and refrigerate 8 hours, or overnight. When ready to serve, warm in the microwave for 1 minute.

GLUTEN FREE: Use GF oats

NUTRITIONAL ANALYSIS

SERVING SIZE: 1½ cups (348 g)

PER SERVING: 410 calories; 5 g fat; 53 g protein; 45 g carbohydrate; 5 g dietary fiber

CHOCOLATE BANANA OVERNIGHT OATS

YIELD:
1 SERVING

PREP TIME:
5 MINUTES

Protein powders come in various flavors. Feel free to substitute a chocolate version instead of the vanilla; just be sure to skip the cocoa powder.

½ cup (40 g) old-fashioned rolled oats
½ cup (118 ml) nonfat milk
½ cup (118 g) plain nonfat Greek yogurt
1 scoop vanilla protein powder
2 teaspoons (4 g) cocoa powder
1 small banana, sliced

In a jar or bowl with a lid, stir oats, milk, yogurt, protein powder, and cocoa powder. Top with banana. Cover and refrigerate 8 hours, or overnight.

NUTRITIONAL ANALYSIS

SERVING SIZE: 1½ cups (446 g)

PER SERVING: 400 calories; 5 g fat; 32 g protein; 68 g carbohydrate; 8 g dietary fiber

PB&J YOGURT PARFAIT

YIELD:
1 SERVING

PREP TIME:
5 MINUTES

Substitute any type of berry you like for the raspberries in this recipe, and feel free to try almond powder and sliced almonds instead of the peanut butter powder and peanuts. While you have your ingredients out, set up an assembly line to make multiple jars and store them in the fridge for grab-and-go breakfasts.

---

1 cup (235 g) plain nonfat Greek yogurt

2 tablespoons (10 g) peanut butter powder

½ cup (114 g) raspberries

1 tablespoon (7 g) roasted peanuts

In a small bowl, stir yogurt and powdered peanut butter until combined. In a mason jar, alternate layers of yogurt with layers of raspberries. Top with peanuts.

GLUTEN FREE

VEGETARIAN

NUTRITIONAL ANALYSIS

SERVING SIZE: 1½ cups (321 g)

PER SERVING: 280 calories; 7 g fat; 31 g protein; 24 g carbohydrate; 8 g dietary fiber

TURKEY "SAUSAGE" HASH

YIELD: 4 SERVINGS

PREP TIME: 10 MINUTES

COOK TIME: 15 MINUTES

Adding sage and a few other spices to basic ground turkey turns it into a surprising approximation of sausage, without all the fat.

- **1 pound (454 g) 93% lean ground turkey**
- **½ teaspoon salt**
- **½ teaspoon ground sage**
- **½ teaspoon thyme**
- **½ teaspoon garlic powder**
- **¼ teaspoon marjoram**
- **¼ teaspoon crushed red pepper flakes**
- **2 medium sweet potatoes, peeled and shredded**
- **1 medium onion, diced**
- **1 green bell pepper, diced**

FOR SERVING

- **4 high-protein bagels (10 g of protein per bagel), toasted if desired**

In a medium bowl, stir turkey, salt, sage, thyme, garlic powder, marjoram, and red pepper flakes. Form turkey mixture into four 4-inch (10-cm)-diameter, ½-inch (1-cm)-thick patties. Heat a skillet sprayed with cooking spray over medium heat. Cook patties 5 to 8 minutes, until browned. Flip and cook 4 to 5 minutes, until the internal temperature reaches 165°F (74°C) and patties are no longer pink in the middle. Remove from pan and set aside.

Spray the same skillet with cooking spray again and add sweet potatoes, onion, and bell pepper. Cook 5 to 8 minutes, until onions are translucent and potatoes are soft. Divide hash between four bowls or meal prep containers, and top with turkey patties. Serve with bagels.

NUTRITIONAL ANALYSIS

SERVING SIZE: 1 turkey patty, ½ cup hash, and 1 bagel (332 g total)

PER SERVING: 490 calories; 11 g fat; 38 g protein; 67 g carbohydrate; 6 g dietary fiber

WARM APPLE CINNAMON OATMEAL

YIELD: 1 SERVING

PREP TIME: 5 MINUTES

COOK TIME: 15 MINUTES

This bowl is perfect for a cozy morning, snuggled up with a book and a cup of tea. Any type of apple works here, and don't worry about peeling it! For a change of pace, substitute ground cardamom for the cinnamon.

½ cup (118 ml) nonfat milk

½ cup (40 g) old-fashioned rolled oats

1 scoop unflavored whey protein powder

¼ teaspoon ground cinnamon

½ apple, cored and shredded on the side of a box grater

1 tablespoon (15 ml) maple syrup

Pinch of salt

1 tablespoon (7 g) chopped walnuts (optional)

In a small saucepan over medium heat, heat milk and ½ cup (118 ml) water until simmering. Stir in oats and cook 3 minutes. Stir in protein powder, cinnamon, apple, syrup, and salt. Cook 3 to 5 minutes, until oatmeal is thickened and apple is soft. Serve topped with walnuts, if desired.

 **GLUTEN FREE:** Use GF oats

NUTRITIONAL ANALYSIS

SERVING SIZE: 1½ cups (415 g; without optional walnuts)

PER SERVING: 400 calories; 4 g fat; 34 g protein; 65 g carbohydrate; 7 g dietary fiber

PROTEIN PANCAKES

- **YIELD:** 1 SERVING
- **PREP TIME:** 10 MINUTES
- **COOK TIME:** 15 MINUTES

Pancakes can be a great item for an on-the-go breakfast. Make a double or triple batch and store them in the fridge for up to three or four days. Substitute bananas or mini chocolate chips for the blueberries if you'd like!

½ cup (60 g) all-purpose flour
1 teaspoon (4 g) baking powder
½ teaspoon ground cinnamon
½ cup (73 g) nonfat cottage cheese
¼ cup (60 ml) nonfat milk
2 large eggs
1 tablespoon (15 ml) maple syrup
1 teaspoon (5 ml) vanilla extract
Pinch of salt
¼ cup (47 g) blueberries

In a medium bowl, whisk flour, baking powder, and cinnamon. In a blender, blend cottage cheese, milk, eggs, maple syrup, vanilla, and salt about 30 seconds, until just combined. Stir wet mixture into the dry and mix just until combined.

Heat a skillet over medium heat and spray with cooking spray. Drop ¼ cups (60 ml) batter onto the hot skillet and cook about 1½ minutes, until bubbles appear at the edge. Flip and cook 2 minutes, until browned on the other side. Serve topped with blueberries.

NUTRITIONAL ANALYSIS

SERVING SIZE: 4 pancakes (363 g)

PER SERVING: 530 calories; 11 g fat; 29 g protein; 78 g carbohydrate; 3 g dietary fiber

CANNOLI BOWL

YIELD:
1 SERVING

PREP TIME:
5 MINUTES

Tired of cottage cheese? Try some ricotta! It has a different texture and is a little sweeter than cottage cheese. We like it because it reminds us of one of our favorite Italian desserts. Hemp seeds are surprisingly high in protein and add a nice crunch.

- **½ cup (124 g) part-skim ricotta cheese**
- **1 scoop unflavored protein powder**
- **1 teaspoon (5 ml) maple syrup**
- **1 tablespoon (15 g) mini chocolate chips**
- **1 teaspoon (3 g) hemp seeds**

In a small bowl, stir ricotta, protein powder, and maple syrup. Alternatively, in a blender, blend for about 30 seconds and then pour into a bowl. Top with chocolate chips and hemp seeds.

VEGETARIAN

NUTRITIONAL ANALYSIS

SERVING SIZE: ¾ cup (173 g)

PER SERVING: 370 calories; 15 g fat; 41 g protein; 19 g carbohydrate; 1 g dietary fiber

OMELET IDEAS

We are big fans of omelets. The flavor combinations are endless, and they are a great way to use up any bits and pieces left in the fridge. This method is pretty basic, with no rolling or other fancy techniques that you might see in some French omelet recipes. As with most egg breakfasts, a slice of toast would be the perfect accompaniment.

Base Recipe

3 large eggs

¼ cup (36 g) nonfat cottage cheese

¼ teaspoon salt

A couple grinds of black pepper

In a blender, blend eggs, cottage cheese, salt, and pepper about 30 seconds, until smooth. Prepare your fillings (see below).

Spray a medium nonstick skillet with cooking spray and heat over medium heat. Pour in egg mixture and swirl to coat the bottom of the pan. Cook, shaking the pan continuously, just until the eggs have set but the top is still a little wet. Sprinkle your chosen fillings on one half of the egg. Carefully fold the other half of the egg over to cover the fillings. Cook 1 to 2 minutes, until the cheese has melted. Slip the omelet onto a plate. Let it sit for 1 to 2 minutes to fully set before serving.

Omelet Ideas (continued on next page)

Western Omelet

- **YIELD:** 1 SERVING
- **PREP TIME:** 10 MINUTES
- **COOK TIME:** 15 MINUTES

1 tablespoon (7 g) chopped bell pepper
1 tablespoon (7 g) chopped onion
1 slice Canadian bacon, chopped
2 tablespoons (14 g) fat-free shredded Cheddar cheese

In a nonstick skillet sprayed with cooking spray over medium heat (this can be the same pan that you are going to cook the eggs in), cook bell pepper and onion 5 to 8 minutes, until softened. Remove from pan and set aside while you cook the eggs.

GLUTEN FREE

VEGETARIAN

NUTRITIONAL ANALYSIS

SERVING SIZE: 1 omelet (276 g)

PER SERVING: 340 calories; 18 g fat; 37 g protein; 7 g carbohydrate; 0 g dietary fiber

Florentine Omelet

- **YIELD:** 1 SERVING
- **PREP TIME:** 10 MINUTES
- **COOK TIME:** 15 MINUTES

¼ cup (39 g) frozen spinach, thawed and drained
¼ cup (28 g) fat-free shredded mozzarella cheese

Place thawed spinach in a kitchen towel and squeeze to drain out as much liquid as possible. Chop spinach into ½-inch (1-cm) pieces. Proceed with cooking the eggs.

GLUTEN FREE

VEGETARIAN

NUTRITIONAL ANALYSIS

SERVING SIZE: 1 omelet (255 g)

PER SERVING: 290 calories; 15 g fat; 33 g protein; 7 g carbohydrate; 1 g dietary fiber

Mushroom Omelet

YIELD: 1 SERVING

PREP TIME: 10 MINUTES

COOK TIME: 15 MINUTES

¼ cup (58 g) mushrooms, fresh or canned and drained

2 tablespoons (14 g) chopped shallot

¼ cup (28 g) fat-free shredded mozzarella cheese

1 teaspoon (1 g) fresh thyme

In a nonstick skillet sprayed with cooking spray over medium heat (this can be the same pan that you are going to cook the eggs in), cook mushrooms and shallot 5 to 8 minutes, until softened. Remove from pan and set aside while you cook the eggs.

GLUTEN FREE

VEGETARIAN

NUTRITIONAL ANALYSIS

SERVING SIZE: 1 omelet (261 g)

PER SERVING: 300 calories; 15 g fat; 33 g protein; 9 g carbohydrate; 1 g dietary fiber

CHEESY GRITS WITH COLLARDS AND CANADIAN BACON

YIELD: 4 SERVINGS

PREP TIME: 10 MINUTES

COOK TIME: 20 MINUTES

A mainstay for breakfast in the American South, grits are a delicious change from your regular oatmeal, especially when cheese is involved. Collards are a great way to get in those leafy greens first thing in the morning and provide a bit of freshness to the meal.

---

2 cups (460 g) chopped collard greens (1 or 2 large leaves)

1 teaspoon (6 g) salt

½ teaspoon oregano

½ teaspoon paprika

¼ teaspoon ground black pepper

4 slices Canadian bacon

4 cups (946 ml) nonfat milk

1 cup (148 g) quick-cooking grits

1 cup (85 g) fat-free shredded Cheddar cheese

1 cup (145 g) nonfat cottage cheese, blended until smooth

Heat a skillet over medium heat and spray with cooking spray. Cook collard greens, salt, oregano, paprika, and pepper 5 minutes, until collards have softened and turned bright green. Push collards to one side of the pan, spray the pan with cooking spray, and add bacon. Cook 1 to 2 minutes, until bacon is crisp and heated through. Set aside while you cook the grits.

In a medium saucepan over medium heat, warm milk. Just as milk begins to bubble, stir in grits. Stir constantly until well combined and grits have no lumps. Reduce heat to low, cover, and simmer gently 5 to 7 minutes, until thickened and creamy. Remove from heat and stir in Cheddar cheese and cottage cheese.

To serve: Divide the grits among four bowls. Top with collards and bacon.

NUTRITIONAL ANALYSIS

SERVING SIZE: ½ cup grits, 1 slice Canadian bacon, and ½ cup collards (396 g total)

PER SERVING: 340 calories; 2 g fat; 31 g protein; 49 g carbohydrate; 2 g dietary fiber

CHAPTER 4

20 Lunches in 30 Minutes

Lunchtime is an opportunity to refuel and recharge with a nutritious meal. It might be easy to forget to eat this one—especially if you used to make your decision to eat based on an obvious hunger signal. You may find it helpful to set a timer or other reminder to take a break and eat. Remember, skipping meals doesn't support your goals for sustainable weight loss and a nutrition plan that meets your protein and fiber goals! Our lunch recipes are designed to be both satisfying and convenient, perfect for busy days when you need a quick and healthy option. From fresh salads to hearty sandwiches, these recipes will keep you energized and focused throughout the afternoon.

TOMATO LENTIL SOUP

Red lentils are one of the fastest-cooking types of lentils and give a nice body to this soup. If you like a little more texture, blend only half of the soup. You may have to add a bit more broth or water to get the consistency you like.

- **YIELD:** 6 SERVINGS
- **PREP TIME:** 5 MINUTES
- **COOK TIME:** 15 MINUTES

---

1 can (14.5 ounces, or 439 g) diced tomatoes with garlic and onion

4 cups (946 ml) chicken bone broth

1½ cups (369 g) dry red lentils, rinsed

1 teaspoon (3 g) cumin

1 teaspoon (6 g) salt

½ teaspoon ground black pepper

2 tablespoons (12 g) chopped cilantro

6 tablespoons (90 g) plain nonfat Greek yogurt

In a large pot, combine tomatoes with their liquid, bone broth, lentils, cumin, salt, and pepper. Bring to a boil. Reduce heat and simmer 10 minutes, until lentils are soft. Remove from heat. Using an immersion blender, blend soup until smooth. Top each serving with cilantro and yogurt, and serve with Greek Yogurt Rolls (See recipe on opposite page).

NUTRITIONAL ANALYSIS

SERVING SIZE: 1 cup (284 g)

PER SERVING: 230 calories; 2 g fat; 19 g protein; 35 g carbohydrate; 6 g dietary fiber

Greek Yogurt Rolls

YIELD: 4 SERVINGS

PREP TIME: 10 MINUTES

COOK TIME: 20 MINUTES

This dough is incredibly versatile and can be made into so many different forms. You'll be amazed! If you have self-rising flour, you can use 1½ cups (180 g) of it and skip the baking powder and salt.

- **1¼ cups (150 g) all-purpose flour**
- **1½ teaspoons (6 g) baking powder**
- **¼ teaspoon salt**
- **1 cup (235 g) plain nonfat Greek yogurt**
- **1 tablespoon (14 g) unsalted butter, melted**

Preheat oven to 400°F (200°C, or gas mark 6). Spray an 8 × 8-inch (20 × 20-cm) cake pan with cooking spray.

In a medium bowl, sift flour, baking powder, and salt. Add yogurt and stir until you have a stiff dough, using a spatula or spoon, then your hands as dough comes together. If dough is sticky, add more flour by the teaspoon until it is workable. Turn dough out onto a floured surface and knead until it is smooth. Divide into eight pieces, roll each piece into a ball, and place in the prepared pan, starting at the center. Brush the tops with melted butter. Bake 20 to 25 minutes, until golden and cooked through, and serve.

NUTRITIONAL ANALYSIS

SERVING SIZE: 2 rolls (101 g)

PER SERVING: 200 calories; 3 g fat; 11 g protein; 33 g carbohydrate; 1 g dietary fiber

BRIGHT ARUGULA SALAD

- **YIELD:** 4 SERVINGS
- **PREP TIME:** 5 MINUTES

Spicy arugula is always a welcome change from boring salad greens and is a lovely complement to any protein. Top each serving with a quick protein of choice: 4 ounces (113 g) of cooked chicken breast (frozen and microwaved works great), a tuna packet, 4 ounces (113 g) of chopped deli turkey, or some air-fried chicken tenders (or a plant-based alternative). Missing the carbs? Throw it in a wrap! The simple dressing can be used on almost any salad and is made with things that are probably already in your pantry and fridge.

¼ cup (60 ml) olive oil

2 tablespoons (30 ml) lemon juice

1 teaspoon (5 ml) Dijon mustard

1 teaspoon (6 g) salt

½ teaspoon ground black pepper

5 ounces (142 g) arugula

¼ cup (30 g) shaved Parmesan cheese

3 tablespoons (30 g) hemp seeds

In a jar with a lid, combine olive oil, lemon juice, mustard, salt, and pepper. Shake vigorously.

In a serving bowl, toss arugula with dressing. Top with Parmesan cheese and hemp seeds.

GLUTEN FREE

VEGETARIAN

NUTRITIONAL ANALYSIS

SERVING SIZE: 1¼ cups (72 g)

PER SERVING: 200 calories; 19 g fat; 6 g protein; 3 g carbohydrate; 1 g dietary fiber

REFRIED BEAN QUESADILLAS

YIELD:
6 SERVINGS

PREP TIME:
10 MINUTES

COOK TIME:
20 MINUTES

Cheese is usually the star of any quesadilla. Although we have definitely included cheese in ours, the refried beans also help with that melty texture and with keeping everything inside your tortilla. You can reduce the amount of cheese if it's giving you the ick and your quesadilla won't totally fall apart.

---

1 red bell pepper, diced

1 small zucchini, diced

½ cup (79 g) corn, fresh or frozen and defrosted

1 can (16 ounces, or 454 g) fat-free refried beans

½ teaspoon salt

¼ teaspoon ground black pepper

6 burrito-sized (10-inch [25-cm]) tortillas (at least 10 g protein each)

1 cup (85 g) shredded fat-free mozzarella cheese

FOR SERVING

½ cup (118 g) plain nonfat Greek yogurt

½ cup (124 g) salsa

2 tablespoons (12 g) chopped cilantro

In a skillet sprayed with cooking spray, cook pepper and zucchini 5 to 8 minutes, until softened. Stir in corn, and cook 1 minute. Add refried beans, salt and pepper, stirring to combine. Remove from heat and wipe out the skillet.

To assemble: Divide bean mixture between six tortillas and top each with mozzarella cheese. Fold each tortilla in half and press lightly to sandwich the ingredients in the middle.

To cook: Spray the skillet with cooking spray. Working in batches, cook quesadillas 3 to 4 minutes, until the bottoms are golden and crispy. Carefully flip quesadillas and cook 2 to 3 minutes, until the other side is golden and the cheese has melted. Repeat with remaining quesadillas.

To serve: Cut each quesadilla into four pieces and serve with Greek yogurt, salsa, and cilantro.

NUTRITIONAL ANALYSIS

SERVING SIZE: 1 quesadilla (283 g)

PER SERVING: 350 calories; 5 g fat; 27 g protein; 49 g carbohydrate; 1 g dietary fiber

SALMON BAGEL CUCUMBER SALAD

YIELD:
1 SERVING

PREP TIME:
10 MINUTES

Social media popularized the idea of eating a whole cucumber—sometimes you just have to! This version is like your favorite loaded bagel order: smoked salmon, a creamy, cheesy dressing, and a little bit of spice.

¾ cup (122 g) nonfat cottage cheese
1 clove garlic, minced
½ teaspoon salt
¼ teaspoon ground black pepper
1 seedless cucumber, thinly sliced
3 ounces (85 g) smoked salmon, chopped
2 tablespoons (14 g) chopped red onion
2 tablespoons (24 g) everything bagel seasoning
1 tablespoon (15 g) capers
1 teaspoon (3 g) chopped jalapeño pepper

In a blender or food processor, blend cottage cheese, garlic, salt, and pepper until smooth. In a 16-ounce (473-ml) container with a lid (a mason jar works well here), combine cucumber, salmon, onion, everything bagel seasoning, capers, and jalapeño. Top with cottage cheese mixture. Close and shake to combine. Serve.

NUTRITIONAL ANALYSIS

SERVING SIZE: 2 cups (429 g)

PER SERVING: 220 calories; 5 g fat; 29 g protein; 18 g carbohydrate; 2 g dietary fiber

COZY AUTUMN ROASTED SALAD

YIELD: 4 SERVINGS

PREP TIME: 10 MINUTES

COOK TIME: 20 MINUTES

Salads with roasted ingredients are perfect for autumn, when root vegetables are abundant and you don't mind turning on the oven. This salad is substantial, a real stick-to-your-ribs meal.

FOR THE SALAD

1 medium sweet potato, peeled and diced

4 cups (510 g) shredded brussels sprouts

1 can (14.5 ounces, or 439 g) chickpeas, drained and rinsed

1 teaspoon (5 g) garlic powder

1 teaspoon (6 g) salt

½ teaspoon ground black pepper

16 ounces (454 g) sliced deli turkey, cut into ½-inch (1-cm) pieces

¼ cup (28 g) reduced-fat feta cheese

¼ cup (30 g) dried cranberries

¼ cup (30 g) unsalted pepitas

FOR THE DRESSING

2 tablespoons (30 ml) olive oil

1 tablespoon (15 ml) balsamic vinegar

1 teaspoon (5 ml) honey

1 teaspoon (5 ml) Dijon mustard

Preheat oven to 400°F (200°C, or gas mark 6). On a large sheet pan sprayed with cooking spray, toss sweet potato, brussels sprouts, and chickpeas with garlic powder, salt, and pepper. Roast 20 to 25 minutes, until potato is tender. Set aside until cool enough to handle.

Meanwhile, make the dressing. In a small bowl, whisk olive oil, balsamic vinegar, honey, and mustard.

In a large serving bowl, toss sweet potato, brussels sprouts, and chickpeas with turkey, feta, and cranberries. Pour dressing over top. Sprinkle with pepitas, and serve.

NUTRITIONAL ANALYSIS

SERVING SIZE: 1½ cups (418 g)

PER SERVING: 440 calories; 15 g fat; 32 g protein; 45 g carbohydrate; 11 g dietary fiber

HERBY QUINOA SALAD WITH CHICKEN

YIELD: 2 SERVINGS

PREP TIME: 15 MINUTES

COOK TIME: 10 MINUTES

Cooking quinoa in the microwave is fast and easy. You can stir together the dressing and chop the veggies while it's cooking and lunch will be ready in no time.

- **½ cup (70 g) uncooked quinoa**
- **1 tablespoon (15 ml) olive oil**
- **2 teaspoons (10 ml) lemon juice**
- **¼ cup (24 g) chopped Italian parsley**
- **1 tablespoon (3 g) chopped fresh mint**
- **1 tablespoon (3 g) chopped chives**
- **1 teaspoon (6 g) salt**
- **¼ teaspoon ground black pepper**
- **1 medium cucumber, chopped**
- **1 cup (244 g) cherry tomatoes, halved**
- **8 ounces (227 g) grilled boneless skinless chicken breasts**

Rinse quinoa and place in a microwaveable bowl with 1 cup (237 ml) water. Cover with a plate or microwaveable cover, and microwave on high for 6 minutes. Remove the cover, stir, and microwave for 4 minutes, or until most of the seeds have unfurled. Let stand covered for 5 minutes, then fluff quinoa with a fork.

In a serving bowl, whisk olive oil, lemon juice, parsley, mint, chives, salt, and pepper. Toss quinoa in dressing. Add cucumber, tomatoes, and chicken.

NUTRITIONAL ANALYSIS

SERVING SIZE: 2 cups (362 g)

PER SERVING: 390 calories; 13 g fat; 41 g protein; 33 g carbohydrate; 4 g dietary fiber

AIR-FRYER SALMON BITES WITH CHILI OIL CUCUMBER SALAD

YIELD: 4 SERVINGS

PREP TIME: 10 MINUTES

COOK TIME: 15 MINUTES

The air fryer is the best way to get these crispy salmon bites on the table when it's too hot to turn on the oven. A mandoline is the fastest way to get the super-thin cuts of cucumber that somehow make the cucumber salad so much tastier. You can peel the cucumber if you like, but it's not necessary.

1½ pounds (680 g) salmon fillet

2 tablespoons (30 ml) hot honey or regular honey

2 tablespoons (30 ml) soy sauce

2 cloves garlic, minced

½ cup (68 g) bread crumbs

1 teaspoon (5 g) garlic powder

1 teaspoon (3 g) smoked paprika

1 teaspoon (6 g) salt

½ teaspoon ground black pepper

FOR THE SALAD

1 large seedless cucumber, sliced into thin rounds

2 tablespoons (30 ml) rice wine vinegar

1 tablespoon (15 g) chili crisp oil

1 teaspoon (5 ml) soy sauce

1 teaspoon (3 g) sesame seeds

Remove salmon skin and cut fillet into ½-inch (1-cm) chunks. In a medium bowl, combine hot honey, soy sauce, and garlic. Toss salmon pieces in honey mixture and let marinate while you prepare bread crumb coating.

In a medium bowl, combine bread crumbs, garlic powder, smoked paprika, salt, and pepper. Toss salmon in bread crumb mixture, coating evenly.

Preheat an air fryer to 400°F (200°C). Place coated salmon pieces in the air fryer basket in a single layer, working in batches if necessary. Air-fry for 7 minutes, until golden and cooked through.

In a medium bowl, combine cucumber, rice wine vinegar, chili oil, and soy sauce. Stir to coat cucumbers evenly. Sprinkle with sesame seeds before serving.

NUTRITIONAL ANALYSIS

SERVING SIZE: 1 cup salmon bites and ½ cup cucumber salad (268 g)

PER SERVING: 360 calories; 14 g fat; 37 g protein; 22 g carbohydrate; 1 g dietary fiber

BROTHY BEANS AND SAUSAGE

YIELD: 4 SERVINGS

PREP TIME: 10 MINUTES

COOK TIME: 20 MINUTES

The French dish cassoulet was the inspiration for this satisfying dish. Originally considered a "peasant" dish, the real thing includes quite a lot of butter and duck fat, which we've swapped for some smoked turkey and bone broth. Grab a crusty baguette to sop up the sauce.

---

1 medium onion, chopped
2 stalks celery, chopped
1 large carrot, chopped
2 cloves garlic, minced
1 teaspoon (1 g) dried thyme
1 teaspoon (2 g) dried rosemary
1 teaspoon (6 g) salt
½ teaspoon ground black pepper
4 cups (946 ml) chicken bone broth
6 baby golden potatoes
2 cans (15.5 ounces, or 439 g each) cannellini beans, drained and rinsed
1 pound (454 g) hardwood smoked turkey sausage, cut into 1-inch (3-cm) chunks

In a large sauté pan sprayed with cooking spray, cook onion, celery, and carrot over medium heat 5 minutes, until onions are translucent. Add garlic, thyme, rosemary, salt, and pepper, and cook 1 minute. Add broth and potatoes and bring to a boil. Reduce heat and simmer 10 minutes, until potatoes are soft. Add beans and sausage. Cook about 5 minutes, until heated through. Serve with crusty bread or Greek Yogurt Rolls (see recipe, page 67).

NUTRITIONAL ANALYSIS

SERVING SIZE: 2 cups (650 g)

PER SERVING: 480 calories; 15 g fat; 41 g protein; 49 g carbohydrate; 11 g dietary fiber

JAMAICAN JERK BEEF PATTY SKILLET

- **YIELD:** 4 SERVINGS
- **PREP TIME:** 10 MINUTES
- **COOK TIME:** 20 MINUTES

Jamaican beef patties are a popular dish that involves spicy ground beef encased in flaky turmeric-spiced dough. Our skillet version adds a flavorful jerk seasoning with a crispy crust that comes together in a flash. Jerk-style food is a staple in Jamaican cooking and is traditionally pretty spicy! If you like the heat, definitely include the Scotch bonnet peppers. If you can't find them, substitute habanero peppers.

---

1 cup (235 g) plain nonfat Greek yogurt

1¼ cups (150 g) self-rising flour

½ teaspoon turmeric

½ teaspoon curry powder

1 teaspoon (5 ml) vegetable oil

1 pound (454 g) 93% lean ground beef

1 teaspoon (6 g) salt

¼ teaspoon ground black pepper

1 medium onion, chopped

1 yellow bell pepper, chopped

2 Scotch bonnet peppers, chopped and seeded (to taste)

1 cup (260 g) green peas

1 tablespoon (51 g) jerk seasoning

Preheat oven to 350°F (180°C, or gas mark 4).

In a medium bowl, stir yogurt, flour, turmeric, and curry powder until you have a shaggy dough. Transfer dough to a lightly floured surface and knead until smooth. Form the dough into a disc that is about 9 inches (23 cm) wide and ¼ inch (6 mm) thick. Cover with a kitchen towel and set aside while you make the filling.

Heat vegetable oil in a 10-inch (25-cm) cast-iron skillet over medium heat. Add ground beef, salt, and pepper, and cook 5 minutes, until beef is no longer pink. Stir in onion, bell pepper, Scotch bonnet pepper, and peas. Cook 5 to 8 minutes, until vegetables have softened. Stir in jerk seasoning. Place disk of dough on top of beef mixture; it should not overlap the edge of the pan. Transfer to the oven and bake 20 to 25 minutes, until the top is golden and crispy.

NUTRITIONAL ANALYSIS

SERVING SIZE: 1¾ cups (337 g)

PER SERVING: 430 calories; 10 g fat; 36 g protein; 46 g carbohydrate; 4 g dietary fiber

ASIAN TUNA SALAD

YIELD: 2 SERVINGS

PREP TIME: 5 MINUTES

A fun way to eat this is to scoop it up with seaweed snacks, which add a fun crispy texture. You can find them in your supermarket in the Asian food section or sometimes the natural food section.

½ tablespoon (8 ml) soy sauce
½ tablespoon (8 ml) sesame oil
1 teaspoon (5 ml) sriracha
½ teaspoon ground black pepper
2 cans (5 ounces, or 142 g each) tuna packed in water, drained
½ cup (43 g) shelled edamame
½ cup (57 g) grated carrot (about 1 small)
2 scallions, chopped
1 teaspoon (3 g) sesame seeds
Seaweed snacks to serve (optional)

In a medium bowl, stir soy sauce, sesame oil, sriracha, and pepper. Add tuna, edamame, carrots, and scallions, and stir until combined. Sprinkle with sesame seeds. Eat with seaweed snacks, serve over shredded romaine lettuce, or serve in a wrap.

NUTRITIONAL ANALYSIS

SERVING SIZE: 1½ cups (204 g; without optional seaweed snacks)

PER SERVING: 210 calories; 7 g fat; 28 g protein; 10 g carbohydrate; 4 g dietary fiber

LOADED MISO SOUP

- **YIELD:** 4 SERVINGS
- **PREP TIME:** 5 MINUTES
- **COOK TIME:** 20 MINUTES

Miso is a great choice for a sensitive tummy. It's soothing and actually helps *your gut with its probiotics and digestive enzymes. Loading up your soup with tasty bits of noodles, tofu, and veggies is just a way to make it* extra.

- **8 ounces (227 g) dry buckwheat soba noodles**
- **6 cups (1.4 L) chicken bone broth**
- **¼ cup (60 ml) white miso paste**
- **1 cup (120 g) baked tofu, cut into ¼-inch (6-mm) pieces**
- **4 ounces (113 g) shiitake mushrooms, sliced**
- **1 cup (86 g) shelled edamame**
- **4 scallions, chopped**

Cook soba noodles according to package directions. Set aside.

In a large pot, heat bone broth to a simmer. Stir in miso until dissolved. Stir in tofu, shiitake mushrooms, edamame, and reserved soba noodles. Simmer 5 minutes, until heated through. Top with scallions.

NUTRITIONAL ANALYSIS

SERVING SIZE: 2 cups (557 g)

PER SERVING: 450 calories; 8 g fat; 37 g protein; 58 g carbohydrate; 6 g dietary fiber

POTATO LEEK SOUP WITH TURKEY BACON

- **YIELD:** 4 SERVINGS
- **PREP TIME:** 10 MINUTES
- **COOK TIME:** 20 MINUTES

Silken tofu adds protein to this classic soup without sacrificing its smooth texture. A few chives snipped over the top of this soup will brighten the color and the flavor.

- **4 leeks, cleaned and chopped**
- **1½ teaspoons (9 g) salt**
- **3 cloves garlic, minced**
- **¼ teaspoon crushed red pepper flakes**
- **4 russet potatoes, peeled and quartered**
- **4 cups (946 ml) chicken bone broth**
- **8 ounces (227 g) silken tofu**
- **6 slices cooked turkey bacon, crumbled**

In a large pot sprayed with cooking spray, cook leeks and salt over medium heat about 10 minutes, until soft. Stir in garlic and red pepper flakes, and cook 1 minute. Add potatoes and bone broth, and bring to a boil. Reduce heat and simmer about 15 minutes, until potatoes are soft. Remove from heat and stir in silken tofu. Using an immersion blender, puree soup until smooth.

If necessary, add water or milk until desired consistency is reached. Serve topped with crumbled turkey bacon.

NUTRITIONAL ANALYSIS

SERVING SIZE: ¾ cup (542 g)

PER SERVING: 300 calories; 6 g fat; 21 g protein; 44 g carbohydrate; 4 g dietary fiber

BBQ CHICKEN FLATBREADS

Lavash bread can be found in your grocery's bakery section. It makes the perfect base for these fillings. You may be tempted to use sugar-free barbecue sauce, but we urge you to go ahead and use the real stuff: the sugar in the sauce caramelizes better and a little goes a long way.

YIELD: 2 SERVINGS

PREP TIME: 10 MINUTES

COOK TIME: 10 MINUTES

---

2 pieces (2.25 ounces, or 64 g) lavash flatbread

⅓ cup (78 ml) barbecue sauce

1 can (9.75 ounces, or 276 g) canned cooked chicken, drained

¼ small red onion, sliced

½ cup (43 g) shredded fat-free mozzarella cheese

½ avocado, peeled and sliced

Preheat oven to 350°F (180°C, or gas mark 4). Spray a baking sheet with cooking spray.

Place lavash on the baking sheet in one layer. Top with barbecue sauce, chicken, red onion, and mozzarella cheese. Bake 10 minutes, until heated through and the cheese has melted. Top with sliced avocado before serving.

NUTRITIONAL ANALYSIS

SERVING SIZE: 1 flatbread (333 g)

PER SERVING: 420 calories; 10 g fat; 48 g protein; 35 g carbohydrate; 5 g dietary fiber

SANDWICH SHOP CHOPPED SALAD

YIELD: 2 SERVINGS

PREP TIME: 15 MINUTES

This salad is based on a popular sub sandwich shop order. It's a sub without the roll ("in a tub")! Is it a hoagie? A grinder? A torpedo? A sub? No matter what you call it, it has all your favorite components and the classic oregano-laced dressing. Don't forget the napkins!

FOR THE DRESSING

3 tablespoons (45 ml) olive oil

2 tablespoons (30 ml) red wine vinegar

1 teaspoon (1 g) oregano

½ teaspoon salt

¼ teaspoon ground black pepper

FOR THE SALAD

1 head iceberg lettuce, shredded

1 cup (149 g) cherry tomatoes, halved

1 cup (115 g) chopped red onion

¼ cup (30 g) chopped pepperoncini

4 slices fat-free Cheddar cheese, chopped

6 slices deli ham, chopped

6 slices deli turkey, chopped

TO MAKE THE DRESSING

In a 16-ounce (473-ml) jar with a lid, combine olive oil, red wine vinegar, oregano, salt, and pepper. Close the jar tightly and shake 30 seconds, until all ingredients are combined.

TO ASSEMBLE THE SALAD

In two serving bowls, divide lettuce, tomatoes, red onion, pepperoncini, cheese, ham, and turkey. Divide the dressing between the two bowls, and gently stir to coat.

NUTRITIONAL ANALYSIS

SERVING SIZE: 4 cups (576 g)

PER SERVING: 400 calories; 24 g fat; 29 g protein; 20 g carbohydrate; 5 g dietary fiber

TACO BOWL

YIELD:
4 SERVINGS

PREP TIME:
10 MINUTES

COOK TIME:
10 MINUTES

Did you know that the original taco bowl was invented at Disneyland? It was a flour tortilla that was deep-fried into the shape of a bowl and piled full of taco ingredients such as ground beef, cheese, lettuce, and tomato. Who knew? Our taco bowl is only a little bit more modern, with a rice base and probably more spice, but we tip our hats to the originators.

- **1 pound (454 g) 93% lean ground beef**
- **1 can (14.5 ounces, or 439 g) black beans, drained and rinsed**
- **1 package (1 ounce, or 28 g) taco seasoning**
- **2 cups (316 g) cooked white rice**
- **1 cup (159 g) corn**
- **1 cup (248 g) salsa**
- **¼ cup (59 g) plain nonfat Greek yogurt**
- **24 tortilla chips**
- **1 avocado, peeled and sliced**

In a skillet sprayed with cooking spray, cook ground beef, black beans, and taco seasoning over medium heat 8 to 10 minutes, until beef is no longer pink. Set aside.

Divide rice between four bowls or meal prep containers. Top with beef mixture, corn, salsa, yogurt, tortilla chips, and avocado.

GLUTEN FREE: Use GF tortilla chips

NUTRITIONAL ANALYSIS

SERVING SIZE: 2 cups (430 g)

PER SERVING: 560 calories; 17 g fat; 37 g protein; 62 g carbohydrate; 11 g dietary fiber

PEPPERONI PIZZA BAKE

YIELD: 2 SERVINGS

PREP TIME: 10 MINUTES

COOK TIME: 20 MINUTES

This is reminiscent of a deep-dish pizza: lots of soft golden crust, not too much sauce, and classic pepperoni toppings. If you like ham and pineapple on your pizza, though, don't let us stop you!

1¼ cups (150 g) self-rising flour

1 cup (235 g) plain nonfat Greek yogurt

½ cup (118 ml) pizza sauce

16 slices (30 g) turkey pepperoni

½ cup (43 g) fat-free shredded mozzarella cheese

6 leaves fresh basil

Preheat oven to 400°F (200°C, or gas mark 6). Spray two small 4 × 6-inch (10 × 15-cm) glass dishes with cooking spray. Small glass food storage or meal prep containers work well here.

In a medium bowl, sift flour. Add yogurt and stir until you have a stiff dough, using a spatula or spoon, then using your hands as the dough comes together. If dough is sticky, add more flour by the teaspoon until it is workable. Turn dough out onto a floured surface and knead until it is smooth. Divide into two pieces and press into the prepared pans. Top with pizza sauce, pepperoni, and cheese. Bake 20 minutes, or until golden and cooked through. Top with basil before serving.

NUTRITIONAL ANALYSIS

SERVING SIZE: 1 mini pizza (298 g)

PER SERVING: 450 calories; 4 g fat; 34 g protein; 69 g carbohydrate; 2 g dietary fiber

NOTE

If you don't have self-rising flour, you may substitute 1¼ cups (150 g) all-purpose flour, 1½ teaspoons (7 g) baking powder, and ¼ teaspoon fine salt.

EGG ROLL BOWL

- **YIELD:** 4 SERVINGS
- **PREP TIME:** 10 MINUTES
- **COOK TIME:** 10 MINUTES

Usually, you'd find ground pork in your egg roll, but using ground turkey in this dish lightens it up quite a bit. The seasonings and sauce will lend an authentic flavor to any protein.

1 pound (454 g) 99% lean ground turkey

1 bag (14 ounces, or 397 g) shredded coleslaw mix (cabbage and carrots)

1 teaspoon (5 g) onion powder

1 teaspoon (5 g) garlic powder

1 teaspoon (3 g) ground ginger

½ teaspoon crushed red pepper flakes

½ teaspoon salt

¼ teaspoon ground black pepper

FOR THE SAUCE

¼ cup (60 ml) soy sauce

1 tablespoon (15 ml) sriracha hot sauce

1 teaspoon (5 ml) sesame oil

1 teaspoon (5 ml) honey

FOR SERVING

2 cups (390 g) cooked brown rice

2 teaspoons (6 g) sesame seeds (optional)

GLUTEN FREE: Substitute tamari for soy sauce

NUTRITIONAL ANALYSIS

SERVING SIZE: 2 cups (337 g; without optional sesame seeds)

PER SERVING: 300 calories; 4 g fat; 32 g protein; 37 g carbohydrate; 4 g dietary fiber

In a skillet coated with cooking spray over medium heat, cook turkey and coleslaw mix sprinkled with onion powder, garlic powder, ground ginger, red pepper flakes, salt, and pepper 10 minutes, until turkey is no longer pink and cabbage has softened.

To make the sauce: In a small bowl, stir soy sauce, sriracha, sesame oil, and honey.

To serve: Divide everything between four bowls or meal prep containers. Start with the rice at the bottom, then the turkey mixture, and pour the sauce over top. Sprinkle ½ teaspoon sesame seeds over each portion, if desired.

THAI PEANUT CHICKEN SALAD

YIELD: 1 SERVING

PREP TIME: 10 MINUTES

This Thai-inspired salad is so colorful and crunchy, you'll want to make it all week. If you'd like a more portable lunch, roll your salad in a wrap.

½ cup (120 g) shredded napa cabbage

4 ounces (113 g) cooked skinless, boneless chicken breasts

¼ cup (21 g) shelled edamame

¼ cup (67 g) diced mango

¼ cup (28 g) diced red bell pepper

2 tablespoons (30 ml) roasted peanuts

FOR THE DRESSING

1 tablespoon (15 ml) olive oil

2 teaspoons (10 ml) soy sauce

2 teaspoons (10 ml) red wine vinegar

½ teaspoon freshly grated ginger

TO MAKE THE DRESSING

In a small bowl, whisk olive oil, soy sauce, vinegar, and ginger.

TO ASSEMBLE THE SALAD

In a medium bowl, combine cabbage, chicken, edamame, mango, and bell pepper. Toss with dressing and top with peanuts.

GLUTEN FREE: Substitute tamari for soy sauce

NUTRITIONAL ANALYSIS

SERVING SIZE: About 2 cups (308 g)

PER SERVING: 400 calories; 21 g fat; 41 g protein; 16 g carbohydrate; 5 g dietary fiber

TUNA NIÇOISE

YIELD:
1 SERVING

PREP TIME:
10 MINUTES

The Niçoise salad hails from the seaside town of Nice in France, where it is a sort of "kitchen sink" dish that uses readily available ingredients (something that we heartily endorse). It also seems appropriate for us to recommend eating this salad in a baguette! Slice a quarter of a baguette in half, pour the dressing on the bread, and layer the ingredients on top. Bon appétit!

FOR THE DRESSING

1 tablespoon (15 ml) olive oil

1 teaspoon (5 ml) balsamic vinegar

½ teaspoon Dijon mustard

½ teaspoon honey

¼ teaspoon salt

FOR THE SALAD

½ head Bibb lettuce, torn into small pieces

1 can (5 ounces, or 142 g) tuna in water, drained

1 hard-boiled egg, peeled and sliced

1 medium tomato, quartered

½ cup (42 g) green beans, fresh or frozen and thawed

4 pitted kalamata olives

TO MAKE THE DRESSING

In a small bowl, whisk olive oil, balsamic vinegar, mustard, honey, and salt.

TO ASSEMBLE THE SALAD

Arrange lettuce in a medium bowl. Top with tuna, egg, tomato, green beans, and olives. Pour dressing over the salad and toss to coat.

NUTRITIONAL ANALYSIS

SERVING SIZE: About 2 to 2½ cups (470 g)

PER SERVING: 420 calories; 24 g fat; 31 g protein; 17 g carbohydrate; 5 g dietary fiber

VEGGIE SALAD WRAP

YIELD: 1 SERVING

PREP TIME: 10 MINUTES

Wrapping food in other food is nothing new: the folks in Southeast Asia have been making lettuce wraps for thousands of years. You could certainly substitute lettuce for the tortilla wrap here, but you'll miss that extra hit of protein that the tortilla supplies, and let's face it, they just roll better!

---

1 tablespoon (15 ml) tahini
2 teaspoons (10 ml) lemon juice
1 teaspoon (5 ml) Dijon mustard
1 clove garlic, minced
¼ cup (65 g) chickpeas
1 (10-inch, 25-cm) low-carb flour tortilla
2 leaves romaine lettuce, chopped
1 piece (3.5 ounces, or 99 g) baked tofu, sliced, any flavor
1 small cucumber, sliced
¼ cup (28 g) shredded carrot

In a medium bowl, whisk tahini, lemon juice, mustard, and garlic until combined, adding water to thin if necessary. Add chickpeas. Using a fork, lightly mash chickpeas into dressing, stirring them together.

Lay tortilla on a flat surface, spread chickpea mixture in the center, and layer lettuce, tofu, cucumber, and carrot on top. Roll up like a burrito and serve.

VEGAN

NUTRITIONAL ANALYSIS

SERVING SIZE: 1 wrap (458 g)

PER SERVING: 430 calories; 18 g fat; 30 g protein; 55 g carbohydrate; 18 g dietary fiber

CHAPTER 5

20 Dinners in 50 Minutes

Dinner is a time to unwind and enjoy a delicious meal with family or friends. That's assuming your household isn't the chaos that mine usually is in the evenings, between kids' activities and homework! In this chapter, you'll find a selection of dinner recipes that are both comforting and nutritious while keeping your capacity for complexity in mind.

LOAF PAN SHAWARMA CHICKEN

- **YIELD:** 4 SERVINGS
- **PREP TIME:** 2 HOURS (MARINATING TIME)
- **COOK TIME:** 50 MINUTES

This Middle Eastern-inspired chicken is so flavorful, you won't believe it. The secret is in the sauce . . . blending the onion just makes its flavor shine! Oh, and the amazing spice blend, too. Leftovers (if there are any) would make great wraps or sandwiches for lunch the next day.

---

1 medium onion

2 tablespoons (30 g) plain nonfat Greek yogurt

2 tablespoons (33 g) tomato paste

1 tablespoon (15 ml) lemon juice

1 tablespoon (3 g) thyme

1 tablespoon (14 g) garlic powder

1 tablespoon (5 g) crushed red pepper flakes (optional)

1 teaspoon (3 g) smoked paprika

1 teaspoon (6 g) salt

½ teaspoon ground black pepper

1 pound (454 g) skinless, boneless chicken breasts

FOR SERVING

2 cups (390 g) cooked brown rice

¼ cup (2 g) cilantro leaves, chopped

In a food processor, blend onion into a paste. Transfer onion to a large bowl or pan with a lid, and stir in yogurt, tomato paste, lemon juice, thyme, garlic powder, red pepper flakes (if using), smoked paprika, salt, and pepper. Stir until well combined. Add chicken breasts, turning to coat with onion mixture. Cover and refrigerate for at least 2 hours, or overnight.

Preheat oven to 425°F (220°C, or gas mark 7). Spray a 9 × 5-inch (23 × 13-cm) loaf pan with cooking spray. Layer chicken breasts in the pan, packing them tight. Discard any leftover marinade. Bake about 50 minutes, until internal temperature reaches 165°F (74°C) when measured with a thermometer in the thickest part. Carefully pour out any excess juices and let chicken cool in the pan for 10 minutes. Turn chicken out onto a cutting board and slice through into ¼-inch (6-mm) slices. Serve over rice with cilantro.

NUTRITIONAL ANALYSIS

SERVING SIZE: ½ cup (630 g)

PER SERVING: 340 calories; 5 g fat; 30 g protein; 44 g carbohydrate; 4 g dietary fiber

TAMALE PIE

- **YIELD:** 6 SERVINGS
- **PREP TIME:** 5 MINUTES
- **COOK TIME:** 45 MINUTES

Tamales are a wonderful traditional Mexican dish that usually involves many hands around a table forming packets of delicious meat inside of a corn-based dough. Our version is a one-pan dish with a tasty filling and prepared polenta for the topping, which makes for a much quicker weeknight meal.

---

1 pound (454 g) 93% lean ground beef

1 can (15.5 ounces, or 439 g) pinto beans, drained and rinsed

1 can (15.5 ounces, or 439 g) black beans, drained and rinsed

1 medium zucchini, chopped

1 can (10 ounces, or 283 g) Mexican-style tomatoes

1 cup (159 g) corn kernels, fresh or frozen

1 cup (248 g) medium chunky salsa

2 teaspoons (6 g) chili powder

1 tube (16–18 ounces, or 510 g) prepared polenta, cut into ½-inch (1-cm) slices

1 cup (85 g) shredded fat-free Cheddar cheese

Preheat oven to 400°F (200°C, or gas mark 6). Spray a 9 × 13-inch (23 × 33-cm) baking pan with cooking spray.

In a large pot, cook ground beef 6 to 8 minutes, until no longer pink. Add pinto beans, black beans, zucchini, tomatoes, corn, salsa, and chili powder. Bring to a boil, reduce heat to low, cover, and simmer for 10 minutes. Transfer to the prepared baking dish. Arrange polenta slices on top, overlapping the slices if necessary.

Bake 25 minutes, until bubbly. Remove from oven, sprinkle with cheese, and return to the oven for 5 minutes, until the cheese has melted.

NUTRITIONAL ANALYSIS

SERVING SIZE: 2 cups (418 g)

PER SERVING: 370 calories; 6 g fat; 32 g protein; 45 g carbohydrate; 9 g dietary fiber

SHRIMP PASTA IN FRESH HERB SAUCE

- **YIELD:** 4 SERVINGS
- **PREP TIME:** 10 MINUTES
- **COOK TIME:** 20 MINUTES

High-protein pastas are readily available these days, and they provide an easy way to get extra protein into your diet without changing your favorite recipes. There are many brands out there with varying textures and tastes, so test them out until you find one that you like.

---

8 ounces (224 g) high-protein angel hair pasta (at least 10 g protein per serving)
¼ cup (24 g) chopped fresh parsley
¼ cup (24 g) chopped fresh basil
2 tablespoons (30 ml) olive oil
2 cloves garlic, minced
1 teaspoon (6 g) salt
¼ teaspoon ground black pepper
1½ pounds (680 g) large shrimp, peeled and deveined
2 medium zucchini, cut into ½-inch (1-cm) pieces
Lemon wedges for serving

Cook pasta according to package directions.

In a large bowl, stir parsley, basil, olive oil, garlic, salt, and pepper. Set aside.

In a nonstick skillet sprayed with cooking spray, sauté shrimp over medium heat about 2 minutes per side, until just opaque. Remove shrimp from pan and set aside. Avoid overcooking! In the same skillet, sauté the zucchini about 5 minutes, until softened and beginning to brown.

When pasta is done, drain and add to herb mixture, tossing to coat. Stir in cooked shrimp and zucchini. Serve with lemon wedges.

NUTRITIONAL ANALYSIS

SERVING SIZE: 2 ounces pasta with 6 ounces shrimp (242 g total)

PER SERVING: 390 calories; 10 g fat; 35 g protein; 44 g carbohydrate; 6 g dietary fiber

SEARED SCALLOPS

- **YIELD:** 4 SERVINGS
- **PREP TIME:** 5 MINUTES
- **COOK TIME:** 10 MINUTES

Seafood is always the fastest-cooking choice for a weeknight protein. Here, buttery scallops are perfectly contrasted against a bright green sauce that's perfect for sopping up with a crusty baguette or a hunk of sourdough bread, so don't forget to visit the bakery while shopping!

---

2 cups (340 g) frozen shelled edamame

1 cup (8 ounces, or 240 ml) chicken bone broth

1 teaspoon (6 g) salt

½ teaspoon ground black pepper

1 teaspoon (5 g) garlic powder

16 large scallops (about 1½ pounds, or 680 g), patted dry

Lemon wedges for serving

In a microwave, defrost edamame with 1 to 2 tablespoons (15 to 30 ml) water, cooking in 1-minute intervals until tender and warmed through. Drain and reserve ¼ cup (383 g) edamame.

In a blender, puree remaining edamame, bone broth, salt and pepper, and garlic powder until smooth, adding water if necessary to achieve a pourable consistency. Cover and set aside while you cook the scallops.

Sprinkle scallops with salt. In a nonstick skillet sprayed with cooking spray and working in batches, sear scallops until golden brown and just translucent in the center, about 2 minutes per side. Transfer to a plate and cover with foil while you cook the remaining scallops.

To serve: Warm edamame puree if necessary. Divide between four plates and top with four scallops each. Sprinkle reserved edamame on top, and serve with lemon wedges.

NUTRITIONAL ANALYSIS

SERVING SIZE: 4 scallops and ½ cup puree (199 g total)

PER SERVING: 140 calories; 5 g fat; 19 g protein; 14 g carbohydrate; 4 g dietary fiber

NOTE

No scallops, no problem! Shrimp or the white fish of your choice are simple substitutes.

CREAMY MUSHROOM PASTA

- **YIELD:** 4 SERVINGS
- **PREP TIME:** 10 MINUTES
- **COOK TIME:** 20 MINUTES

Tempeh is a fermented soy product that is often used to mimic meat in vegetarian dishes. Its nutty taste and crumbly texture go well with the earthy mushrooms in this dish. A bonus is that the fermentation makes tempeh easier to digest than other meat substitutes, and we love to be gut-healthy!

---

8 ounces (227 g) chickpea penne or other high-protein pasta (10 g protein per 2-ounce serving)

1 medium onion, chopped

3 cloves garlic, chopped

8 ounces (227 g) mushrooms, chopped

1 package (8 ounces, or 227 g) tempeh, crumbled or cut into ½-inch (1-cm) pieces

1 teaspoon (6 g) salt, divided

⅛ teaspoon ground black pepper

16 ounces (454 g) silken tofu

2 tablespoons (6 g) nutritional yeast

2 teaspoons (10 ml) lemon juice

1½ teaspoons (13 g) Italian seasoning

¼ teaspoon crushed red pepper flakes

Cook pasta according to package directions. When pasta is done, drain and reserve about ½ cup (118 ml) cooking water.

While pasta is cooking, make the sauce: In a large skillet sprayed with cooking spray, cook onion and garlic over medium heat 5 to 8 minutes, until soft. Remove from pan and set aside.

In the same pan, cook mushrooms, tempeh, ½ teaspoon salt, and pepper 10 to 12 minutes, until mushrooms have released all their water and the pan is looking dry.

Meanwhile, in a blender, blend silken tofu, nutritional yeast, lemon juice, the remaining ½ teaspoon salt, Italian seasoning, red pepper flakes, and cooked onion and garlic until smooth. If you like a thinner sauce, add reserved pasta water by the tablespoon until desired consistency is reached. Once the mushrooms are cooked, turn the heat to low, and add sauce and drained pasta to the pan. Stir and cook 1 minute to warm through.

NUTRITIONAL ANALYSIS

SERVING SIZE: 1½ cups (324 g)

PER SERVING: 400 calories; 13 g fat; 33 g protein; 45 g carbohydrate; 7 g dietary fiber

WHITE CHICKEN CHILI

- **YIELD:** 6 SERVINGS
- **PREP TIME:** 10 MINUTES
- **COOK TIME:** 20 MINUTES

As with most chilis, this one tastes better the next day. If you like a creamier texture, blend one of the cans of beans until smooth before stirring it into the chili. You can go hog wild with toppings: try cilantro, chopped scallions, a dollop of plain Greek yogurt, some shredded cheese, or even some crumbled bacon.

---

1 large onion, chopped

2 cloves garlic, minced

1 pound (454 g) boneless, skinless chicken breasts, cut into ½-inch (1-cm) pieces

3 cups (710 ml) chicken bone broth

2 cans (4 ounces, or 113 g each) diced green chiles

1 tablespoon (9 g) chili powder

1½ teaspoons (4 g) ground cumin

1 teaspoon (6 g) salt

1 teaspoon (1 g) oregano

½ teaspoon ground black pepper

¼ teaspoon cayenne

2 cans (15.5 ounces, or 439 g each) white beans, rinsed and drained

1 cup (159 g) corn, fresh or frozen

In a large pot sprayed with cooking spray, cook onion and garlic 5 minutes, until soft. Add chicken, bone broth, green chiles, chili powder, cumin, salt, oregano, pepper, and cayenne. Simmer about 15 minutes, until chicken is no longer pink. Stir in beans and corn and cook about 10 minutes, until warmed through.

GLUTEN FREE

NUTRITIONAL ANALYSIS

SERVING SIZE: 1¾ cups (364 g)

PER SERVING: 330 calories; 9 g fat; 31 g protein; 32 g carbohydrate; 7 g dietary fiber

GRILLED FLANK STEAK WITH CHIMICHURRI RICE

YIELD: 4 SERVINGS

PREP TIME: 10 MINUTES

COOK TIME: 15 MINUTES

Flank steak is a lean cut of beef, so it's quick-cooking and can often benefit from a sauce like Argentinian chimichurri, which is fresh, herby, and spicy. If you've never grilled scallions before, be prepared to have a new favorite: the grill turns them from a basic vegetable into a soft, sweet, satisfying side dish.

FOR THE CHIMICHURRI SAUCE

- 1 cup (96 g) chopped cilantro
- 1 cup (96 g) chopped fresh parsley
- 1 cup (115 g) chopped red onion
- 2 tablespoons (30 ml) olive oil
- 2 tablespoons (30 ml) apple cider vinegar
- 1 clove garlic, minced
- 1 teaspoon (6 g) salt
- ¼ teaspoon crushed red pepper flakes
- ¼ teaspoon ground black pepper

FOR THE STEAK

- 1 teaspoon (5 g) garlic powder
- 1 teaspoon (3 g) cumin
- ½ teaspoon dried oregano
- 1 teaspoon (6 g) salt
- ½ teaspoon ground black pepper
- 1½–2 pounds (680–907 g) flank steak
- 12 scallions
- 16 asparagus spears, trimmed
- 2 cups (348 g) cooked white rice

TO MAKE THE SAUCE

In a medium bowl, stir cilantro, parsley, red onion, olive oil, apple cider vinegar, 1 tablespoon (15 ml) water, garlic, salt, red pepper flakes, and black pepper.

TO MAKE THE STEAK

Heat a grill or grill pan to high. In a small bowl, stir garlic powder, cumin, oregano, salt, and pepper. Rub spice mixture all over flank steak. Grill steak to desired doneness, 3 to 4 minutes for medium-rare on each side. Add scallions and asparagus to the grill and cook about 2 minutes per side, until softened.

TO SERVE

Stir half the chimichurri sauce into cooked rice. Slice flank steak against the grain into ¼-inch (1-cm) slices. Serve steak with rice, grilled scallions, and asparagus, topped with the remaining chimichurri sauce.

GLUTEN FREE

NUTRITIONAL ANALYSIS

SERVING SIZE: 2 cups (377 g)

PER SERVING: 470 calories; 18 g fat; 43 g protein; 34 g carbohydrate; 5 g dietary fiber

SHEET PAN BBQ PORK TENDERLOIN

- **YIELD:** 4 SERVINGS
- **PREP TIME:** 5 MINUTES
- **COOK TIME:** 25 MINUTES

The pork gets a double-whammy of flavor when you use your favorite barbecue rub and then brush it with barbecue sauce. If you like to dip your vegetables (and who doesn't?), try the creamy ranch sauce. It will complement the barbecue flavors perfectly.

---

1 (1–1½ pounds, or 454–680 g) pork tenderloin, trimmed of excess fat

1 tablespoon (7 g) dry barbecue rub

1 pound (454 g) sweet potatoes, cut into ½-inch (1-cm) pieces

½ pound (227 g) green beans, trimmed

½ teaspoon salt

½ teaspoon ground black pepper

½ cup (118 ml) barbecue sauce

Preheat oven to 425°F (220°C, or gas mark 7). Line a 12 × 18–inch (30 × 46–cm) sheet pan with parchment paper.

Season pork with barbecue rub, salt, and pepper, pressing to adhere spices to pork. Place pork in the middle of the prepared pan and surround with sweet potatoes and green beans. Lightly spray sweet potatoes and green beans with cooking spray and season everything with salt and pepper. Bake 25 to 30 minutes, until pork reaches an internal temperature of 145°F (63°C). Brush pork with barbecue sauce before serving.

GLUTEN FREE

NUTRITIONAL ANALYSIS

SERVING SIZE: 2 cups (377 g)

PER SERVING: 360 calories; 4 g fat; 39 g protein; 42 g carbohydrate; 5 g dietary fiber

NOTE

Although you may have used sugar-free barbecue sauce in the past, go ahead and use the real thing here. A little bit will go a long way, and more flavor means you're more likely to eat what you need.

BUTTERNUT SQUASH PASTA BAKE

- **YIELD:** 6 SERVINGS
- **PREP TIME:** 15 MINUTES
- **COOK TIME:** 15 MINUTES

When mac and cheese sounds just a bit too rich, but you still want that comforting cheesy goodness, try this pasta bake! The butternut squash and the beans provide lots of nutrients while the mozzarella will still give you a photo-worthy cheese pull.

---

1 box (14.5 ounces, or 411 g) high-protein elbow pasta (10 g protein per 2-ounce serving)

1 cup (145 g) nonfat cottage cheese

1 can (14.5 ounces, or 439 g) white beans, such as cannellini, undrained

1 can (15 ounces, or 425 g) butternut squash puree

1 teaspoon (1 g) dried thyme

1 teaspoon (1 g) dried oregano

1 teaspoon (5 g) garlic powder

1 teaspoon (6 g) salt

1¾ cups (7 ounces, or 198 g) shredded fat-free mozzarella cheese

¼ cup (30 g) shredded Parmesan cheese

Preheat oven to 350°F (180°C, or gas mark 4). Spray a 9 × 13–inch (23 × 33–cm) pan with cooking spray.

Cook pasta in a large pot according to package directions. Drain and return to the pot.

In a blender, blend cottage cheese until smooth. Add undrained can of beans and blend again until smooth. Add butternut squash, thyme, oregano, garlic powder, and salt, and blend until combined. Pour sauce over pasta, and stir to combine. Stir in mozzarella. Pour pasta mixture into the prepared pan. Sprinkle Parmesan cheese on top and bake about 15 minutes, until the top is browned and the cheese is melted.

VEGETARIAN

NUTRITIONAL ANALYSIS

SERVING SIZE: 2½ cups (270 g)

PER SERVING: 470 calories; 7 g fat; 33 g protein; 74 g carbohydrate; 12 g dietary fiber

NOTE

If you can't find canned butternut squash, look for frozen butternut squash puree or substitute a can of plain pumpkin puree (not pumpkin pie filling).

SLOW COOKER CUBAN PORK TENDERLOIN WITH 1905 SALAD

YIELD: 6 SERVINGS

PREP TIME: 10 MINUTES

COOK TIME: 4 HOURS (UNATTENDED)

This classic Cuban dish is usually made with a fattier cut of pork, but we're keeping it lean here with the tenderloin. Serve this with a side of yellow rice, black beans, and the iconic 1905 Salad (recipe on opposite page).

---

1 tablespoon (15 ml) olive oil
6 cloves garlic, minced
⅓ cup (78 ml) lime juice
⅓ cup (78 ml) orange juice
⅓ cup (78 ml) grapefruit juice
1 tablespoon (15 ml) yellow mustard
1 tablespoon (24 g) lime zest
1 tablespoon (24 g) orange zest
2 teaspoons (6 g) cumin
2 teaspoons (2 g) oregano
1 teaspoon (6 g) salt
½ teaspoon ground black pepper
¼ teaspoon crushed red pepper flakes
1 (2-pound [907-g]) pork tenderloin, trimmed of excess fat

In a slow cooker, stir olive oil, garlic, lime juice, orange juice, grapefruit juice, mustard, lime zest, orange zest, cumin, oregano, salt, pepper, and red pepper flakes. Add pork tenderloin, making sure to coat the pork in the wet mixture. Close the lid and cook on low about 4 hours, until the internal temperature of the meat reaches 145°F (63°C). Remove pork and let it rest for 10 minutes before slicing. You can use the juices from the slow cooker as a sauce, if desired.

NUTRITIONAL ANALYSIS

SERVING SIZE: 2 cups (174 g)

PER SERVING: 190 calories; 5 g fat; 32 g protein; 3 g carbohydrate; 0 g dietary fiber

1905 Salad

YIELD:
4 SERVINGS

PREP TIME:
10 MINUTES

This salad is adapted from the Columbia Restaurant chain in Tampa, Florida, where it has been a staple menu item since the 1970s. Because sometimes you just need that cool crisp iceberg lettuce and a tangy, uncomplicated dressing to make you feel like you're in the tropics!

FOR THE DRESSING

¼ cup (60 ml) olive oil

2 tablespoons (30 ml) white vinegar

4 cloves garlic, minced

2 teaspoons (10 ml) fresh lemon juice

1 teaspoon (5 ml) Worcestershire sauce

1 teaspoon (1 g) dried oregano

1 teaspoon (6 g) salt

½ teaspoon ground black pepper

FOR THE SALAD

1 head iceberg lettuce, shredded

2 medium tomatoes, cut into eighths

4 ounces (113 g) low-fat Swiss cheese, cut into ¼-inch (6-mm) cubes

4 ounces (113 g) sliced ham, cut into ¼-inch (6-mm) strips

16 pitted green manzanilla olives

2 teaspoons (5 g) freshly grated Parmesan cheese

TO MAKE THE DRESSING

In an 8-ounce (237-ml) jar with a lid, combine olive oil, white vinegar, garlic, lemon juice, Worcestershire sauce, oregano, salt, and pepper. Close the jar and shake vigorously to combine.

TO ASSEMBLE THE SALAD

In a serving bowl, combine iceberg lettuce, tomatoes, Swiss cheese, ham, and olives. Toss. Pour dressing over top and toss once more. Top with the Parmesan cheese.

NUTRITIONAL ANALYSIS

SERVING SIZE: 2 cups salad and 2 tablespoons dressing (306 g total)

PER SERVING: 260 calories; 18 g fat; 15 g protein; 10 g carbohydrate; 2 g dietary fiber

SMASH BURGERS WITH AIR-FRIED POTATO WEDGES AND BURGER SAUCE

YIELD: 4 SERVINGS

PREP TIME: 10 MINUTES

COOK TIME: 20 MINUTES

Smash burgers are all the rage for a reason: the thin patties take no time to cook but still have all the flavor of your favorite hamburger. The air fryer makes crispy potato wedges do-able in half the time it would take to bake them in the oven: win!

---

2 large russet potatoes, cut into wedges

½ teaspoon salt, plus more for seasoning

⅛ teaspoon ground black pepper

1 pound (454 g) 93% lean ground beef

4–8 slices Cheddar cheese (optional)

4 sesame hamburger buns

1 large tomato, sliced

4 leaves butter lettuce

Burger Sauce (optional; recipe on opposite page)

Preheat an air fryer to 400°F (200°C). Spray the basket or tray with cooking spray and add potato wedges in one layer, working in batches if necessary. Spray potatoes lightly with cooking spray and season with salt and pepper. Air-fry about 20 minutes, until golden and crispy, stopping halfway through to shake the basket or flip the potatoes. Meanwhile, make burgers.

Divide ground beef into eight pieces and form each piece into a rough ball shape. To avoid tough patties, don't handle the beef too much; just get it into a general shape. Heat a large skillet or griddle over medium heat. Spray with cooking spray and working in batches, place one piece of beef in the pan. Cover with a square of parchment paper (about 6 inches [15 cm] square) and using a burger press or the bottom of a large can, smash the burger down to flatten it. Remove the parchment paper and sprinkle the burger with a little bit of salt. Repeat with remaining beef, being sure not to crowd the pan. After about 2 minutes, when patties are crispy on the edges, flip and cook on the other side for another minute. If you are using cheese, add the cheese now.

Serve two patties on a bun with tomato, lettuce, and Burger Sauce, if desired.

GLUTEN FREE: Use GF buns

NUTRITIONAL ANALYSIS

SERVING SIZE: 1 burger (420 g; without optional cheese)

PER SERVING: 500 calories; 12 g fat; 33 g protein; 67 g carbohydrate; 4 g dietary fiber

Burger Sauce

- **YIELD:** 4 SERVINGS
- **PREP TIME:** 5 MINUTES

You know you have all these condiments in your fridge, so why not use them? The more, the merrier!

¼ cup (59 g) plain nonfat Greek yogurt
2 tablespoons (30 ml) ketchup
1 tablespoon (15 ml) dill pickle relish
1 teaspoon (5 ml) yellow mustard
½ teaspoon vinegar
½ teaspoon garlic powder
½ teaspoon salt
¼ teaspoon ground black pepper

In a medium bowl, stir yogurt, ketchup, relish, mustard, vinegar, garlic powder, salt, and pepper until combined.

NUTRITIONAL ANALYSIS

SERVING SIZE: 2 tablespoons (29 g)

PER SERVING: 20 calories; 0 g fat; 2 g protein; 3 g carbohydrate; 0 g dietary fiber

3 THINGS TO DO WITH ROTISSERIE CHICKEN

Almost all grocery stores sell rotisserie chickens these days, and they are not only delicious but very versatile. Here are three ideas for your next chicken adventure!

Broccoli Chicken Alfredo

- **YIELD:** 4 SERVINGS
- **PREP TIME:** 10 MINUTES
- **COOK TIME:** 15 MINUTES

Cottage cheese is the hardest-working ingredient in the high-protein diet, for sure! Here, it brings that silky texture to our lightened Alfredo-style sauce without adding lots of fat.

8 ounces (227 g) high-protein pasta (10 g protein per 2-ounce serving), any shape

1 cup (237 ml) nonfat milk

½ cup (73 g) nonfat cottage cheese

½ cup (60 g) grated Parmesan cheese

2 teaspoons (5 g) cornstarch

2 cloves garlic, minced

1 bag (12 ounces, or 340 g) frozen broccoli florets, defrosted

3 cups (420 g) chicken meat, picked from 1 rotisserie chicken

1 teaspoon (6 g) salt

½ teaspoon ground black pepper

3 or 4 sprigs fresh basil for garnish

Cook pasta according to package directions. Meanwhile, make the sauce.

In a blender, blend milk, cottage cheese, Parmesan cheese, cornstarch, and garlic until smooth. Pour sauce into a large saucepan and heat over medium heat 5 to 8 minutes, until thickened. Stir in broccoli, chicken, and cooked pasta, coating everything with sauce. Heat about 5 minutes, until warmed through. Serve garnished with fresh basil.

NUTRITIONAL ANALYSIS

SERVING SIZE: 2 cups (327 g)

PER SERVING: 420 calories; 8 g fat; 43 g protein; 52 g carbohydrate; 8 g dietary fiber

Chicken Caesar Kale Salad

YIELD:
4 SERVINGS

PREP TIME:
15 MINUTES

It may seem weird to massage the dressing into the kale, but it really helps soften the kale's texture. Using prepared dressing and croutons allows you to get this dinner on the table in no time.

1 bunch (½ pound, or 450 g) lacinato kale

½ cup (118 g) lite Caesar salad dressing

3 cups (420 g) chicken meat, picked from 1 rotisserie chicken

1 cup (56 g) seasoned croutons

1 cup (120 g) shaved Parmesan cheese

Remove thick ribs from kale and cut into 1-inch (3-cm) pieces. Put kale into a serving dish, add salad dressing, and massage. Add chicken, croutons, and Parmesan cheese, and toss to coat.

GLUTEN FREE: Use GF croutons

NUTRITIONAL ANALYSIS

SERVING SIZE: 2 cups (228 g)

PER SERVING: 420 calories; 23 g fat; 40 g protein; 16 g carbohydrate; 1 g dietary fiber

3 Things to Do with Rotisserie Chicken (continued on next page)

Pesto Chicken with Spaghetti Squash

- **YIELD:** 4 SERVINGS
- **PREP TIME:** 10 MINUTES
- **COOK TIME:** 40 MINUTES

If you grow your own basil in your garden or on your windowsill, you have probably made pesto several times. It freezes well, so you probably also know the absolute joy of the summery taste of pesto in the depths of winter. Feel free to use homemade in this recipe!

- **1 medium (approximately 3 pounds, or 1.3 kg) spaghetti squash, halved and seeds removed**
- **3 cups (420 g) chicken meat, picked from 1 rotisserie chicken**
- **½ cup (118 ml) prepared pesto**
- **1 cup (149 g) cherry tomatoes, halved**

Preheat oven to 400°F (200°C, or gas mark 6). Spray a baking sheet with cooking spray.

Arrange spaghetti squash, cut side down, on the baking sheet and roast about 40 minutes, until soft and beginning to brown. Let sit until cool enough to handle. Using a fork, scrape out the flesh of the squash, letting it separate into spaghetti-like strands, into a serving bowl. Add pesto and toss until squash is coated evenly. Add chicken and cherry tomatoes, and serve.

NUTRITIONAL ANALYSIS

SERVING SIZE: 1¾ cups (517 g)

PER SERVING: 400 calories; 22 g fat; 33 g protein; 32 g carbohydrate; 5 g dietary fiber

AIR-FRYER TOFU WITH CUCUMBER CELERY SALAD

YIELD: 2 SERVINGS

PREP TIME: 15 MINUTES

COOK TIME: 15 MINUTES

Cooking tofu in the air fryer makes it extra crispy and may help you get over that "I hate tofu" hang-up. Don't skip pressing the tofu; it really helps it absorb all the delicious flavors of the marinade.

- **1 package (16 ounces, or 453 g) extra-firm tofu, drained**
- **1 tablespoon (15 ml) toasted sesame oil**
- **3 tablespoons (45 ml) soy sauce**
- **3 cloves garlic, minced**
- **2 tablespoons (27 g) grated fresh ginger**
- **1 teaspoon (5 g) chili crisp**
- **1 medium cucumber, peeled and sliced into thin rounds**
- **2 stalks celery, sliced into thin pieces**
- **1 tablespoon (8 g) cornstarch**

Press tofu to remove excess liquid: Wrap block of tofu in two layers of paper towels and press under a heavy cast-iron skillet for 15 minutes. Remove the skillet and paper towels. Cut tofu into ½-inch (1-cm) cubes.

In a medium bowl, stir oil, soy sauce, garlic, ginger, and chili crisp. Reserve half the mixture in a second medium bowl. Add cucumber and celery, and stir to combine. Set aside.

Toss tofu cubes in the remaining sesame mixture. Sprinkle cornstarch over tofu and toss again. Preheat an air fryer to 400°F (200°C). Working in batches, air-fry tofu 12 to 15 minutes in a single layer until crispy and golden, stirring tofu halfway through. Serve crispy tofu with celery and cucumber salad.

NUTRITIONAL ANALYSIS

SERVING SIZE: 2 cups (386 g)

PER SERVING: 330 calories; 19 g fat; 23 g protein; 18 g carbohydrate; 4 g dietary fiber

STEAK FAJITAS WITH AIR-FRIED PLANTAINS

- **YIELD:** 4 SERVINGS
- **PREP TIME:** 15 MINUTES
- **COOK TIME:** 20 MINUTES

Who can forget the sound (and smell) of the sizzling fajita skillet making its way through the restaurant to your table? There's something so fun about a meal where you get to create your own experience, such as with tacos or fajitas, not to mention how great it tastes!

---

2 very ripe plantains
1 tablespoon (15 ml) vegetable oil
1 tablespoon (15 ml) lime juice
1 clove garlic, minced
½ teaspoon chili powder
½ teaspoon cumin
½ teaspoon crushed red pepper flakes
½ teaspoon salt
1 pound (454 g) top sirloin steak, sliced into ½-inch (1-cm) strips
2 medium onions, sliced into ½-inch (1-cm) strips
2 bell peppers, any color, sliced into ½-inch (1-cm) strips
8 flour tortillas (6 inches, 15 cm)

Preheat an air fryer to 375°F (190°C). Spray the basket or tray with cooking spray. Peel plantains and slice into 1-inch (3-cm) pieces. Place plantain slices into the air fryer in a single layer and spray lightly with cooking spray. Cook about 16 minutes, or until tender and golden brown, turning them once halfway through. While plantains are cooking, make fajitas.

In a medium bowl, stir vegetable oil, lime juice, garlic, chili powder, cumin, red pepper flakes, and salt. Add beef slices to marinade and stir to coat.

In a large skillet sprayed with cooking spray over medium heat, cook onion and pepper slices 4 to 5 minutes, until softened. Add beef and its marinade to the skillet and cook until desired doneness, 3 to 4 minutes for medium-rare.

To serve: Place a portion of beef, onion, and pepper mixture onto each tortilla. Add toppings as desired, and serve with plantains.

GLUTEN FREE: Use GF tortillas

NUTRITIONAL ANALYSIS

SERVING SIZE: 2 fajitas and ½ plantain (433 g total)

PER SERVING: 630 calories; 17 g fat; 35 g protein; 93 g carbohydrate; 8 g dietary fiber

SIMPLE POACHED CHICKEN

YIELD: 4 SERVINGS

PREP TIME: 5 MINUTES

COOK TIME: 20 MINUTES

Poaching is one of the easiest ways to cook chicken. You can flavor the water any way you want: instead of the lemon, try adding herbs (e.g., rosemary, dill, parsley) or ginger and garlic. Whatever fits the dish you are making!

- **1 pound (454 g) boneless, skinless chicken breasts, cut into 4-ounce (113-g) pieces**
- **1 lemon, halved**
- **1 teaspoon (6 g) salt**
- **1 teaspoon (3 g) ground black pepper**

In a large pot, combine chicken, lemon, salt, and pepper. Add enough water to cover the ingredients. Heat on high until water comes to a boil, skimming off any white foam that appears on the top of the water. Once the water is boiling, remove the pot from the heat, cover, and let sit for 5 minutes. Using a thermometer, measure the temperature of the chicken; it should be at least 165°F (74°C). If it needs more time, cover, wait 5 minutes, and measure again. Remove chicken and use as desired, discarding lemon and cooking liquid.

NUTRITIONAL ANALYSIS

SERVING SIZE: ¾ cup (113 g)

PER SERVING: 140 calories; 3 g fat; 26 g protein; 0 g carbohydrate; 0 g dietary fiber

NOTE

Poached chicken is great when your stomach doesn't want anything too complicated. To make this a complete meal, pair it with a simple cooked vegetable such as green beans or carrots (frozen options work well here) and a cup of cooked white rice. You could also shred the chicken and add it to a cup of chicken broth with some noodles and mixed vegetables for a chicken noodle soup.

SLOW COOKER GARLIC ROSEMARY CHICKEN

YIELD: 4 SERVINGS

PREP TIME: 10 MINUTES

COOK TIME: 4 HOURS

Comforting, easy, and flavorful, this slow cooker dish ticks all the boxes. To switch things up a bit, try it with green beans instead of carrots, or skip the potatoes, shred the chicken, and serve over some fluffy quinoa.

- 1 cup (237 ml) chicken bone broth
- 4 cloves garlic, minced
- 3 tablespoons (45 ml) Worcestershire sauce
- 1 tablespoon (15 ml) Dijon mustard
- 1 tablespoon (18 g) salt
- 2 teaspoons (6 g) ground black pepper
- 2 teaspoons (7 g) onion powder
- 1 teaspoon (2 g) thyme
- 4 boneless, skinless chicken breasts (about 3 ounces, or 85 g each)
- 1 bag (24 ounces, or 680 g) baby golden potatoes
- 3 medium carrots, peeled and cut into 1-inch (3-cm) pieces
- 1 sprig fresh rosemary

In a slow cooker, stir bone broth, garlic, Worcestershire sauce, mustard, salt, pepper, onion powder, and thyme. Place chicken breasts, potatoes, and carrots in the slow cooker and lay the rosemary sprig on top. Cover and cook on low 4 to 5 hours, until potatoes are tender and a thermometer inserted into the thickest part of the chicken registers 165°F (74°C).

NUTRITIONAL ANALYSIS

SERVING SIZE: 2 cups (418 g)

PER SERVING: 330 calories; 4 g fat; 33 g protein; 40 g carbohydrate; 5 g dietary fiber

BREADED CHICKEN TENDERS WITH TZATZIKI

- **YIELD:** 4 SERVINGS
- **PREP TIME:** 20 MINUTES
- **COOK TIME:** 10 MINUTES

Sure, you could bring home a bag of pre-breaded chicken to throw in the air fryer, but this one features no weird ingredients or preservatives and really takes only about fifteen minutes to prepare. Tzatziki is a Greek sauce that's made with (surprise) Greek yogurt, our favorite high-protein ingredient. We've suggested carrots and celery here, but it will pair with whatever fresh veggies you have on hand.

FOR THE CHICKEN

2 large eggs

1 tablespoon (9 g) Italian seasoning

1 cup (136 g) panko bread crumbs

1 pound (454 g) chicken tenders

FOR THE TZATZIKI

1 medium cucumber

1 cup (235 g) plain nonfat Greek yogurt

1 clove garlic, minced

2 tablespoons (1 g) chopped fresh dill

1 teaspoon (6 g) salt

½ teaspoon ground black pepper

FOR SERVING

1 large carrot, cut into 3-inch (8-cm) sticks

2 celery stalks, cut into 3-inch (8-cm) sticks

Preheat an air fryer to 400°F (200°C).

In a shallow bowl, whisk eggs and Italian seasoning. Put bread crumbs in a separate shallow bowl. One at a time, dip chicken tender first into egg, allowing any excess to drip off, then into bread crumbs, rolling to coat all sides. Place breaded chicken on a plate while you repeat the breading process with the remaining chicken.

When all chicken is breaded, place tenders in the air fryer in a single layer and air-fry 8 to 10 minutes, until crispy and golden, stopping to flip the pieces after 5 minutes. Work in batches if you need to, being sure to not crowd the air fryer basket.

To make the tzatziki: Shred the cucumber (peeling is optional) and allow it to drain in a fine-mesh strainer for a few minutes. Press on cucumber to release any excess water. In a medium bowl, stir cucumber, yogurt, garlic, dill, salt, and pepper.

Serve chicken tenders with carrot and celery sticks and tzatziki for dipping.

GLUTEN FREE: Use GF panko bread crumbs

NUTRITIONAL ANALYSIS

SERVING SIZE: ¼ pound chicken tenders, ½ cup tzatziki, 4 carrot sticks, 4 celery sticks (310 g)

PER SERVING: 290 calories; 5 g fat; 39 g protein; 25 g carbohydrate; 3 g dietary fiber

SHAKSHUKA

- **YIELD:** 4 SERVINGS
- **PREP TIME:** 5 MINUTES
- **COOK TIME:** 25 MINUTES

Shakshuka is a popular dish in North Africa and the Middle East that consists of eggs poached in a spiced tomato sauce, cooked on the stovetop. It can be served for breakfast, lunch, or dinner; just be sure to include some pita or a crusty loaf of bread to sop up the delicious sauce.

---

1 medium onion, chopped

1 bell pepper (any color), chopped

1 cup (260 g) canned chickpeas

3 cloves garlic, minced

1 tablespoon (9 g) paprika

1 teaspoon (3 g) cumin

1 teaspoon (2 g) ground coriander

½ teaspoon salt

¼ teaspoon ground black pepper

1 can (28 ounces, or 794 g) crushed tomatoes

8 large eggs

4 whole-wheat pita breads

1 cup (235 g) plain nonfat Greek yogurt

In a large oven-safe skillet or cast-iron skillet sprayed with cooking spray over medium heat, cook onion and pepper 8 to 10 minutes, until softened. Stir in chickpeas, garlic, paprika, cumin, coriander, salt, and pepper, and cook 1 minute. Add crushed tomatoes and simmer 10 minutes, until slightly reduced. Crack eggs into the pan, spacing them evenly. Cover and cook 5 to 8 minutes, until egg whites are set but yolks are still a bit runny. Serve in bowls with a piece of pita bread and ¼ cup (59 g) yogurt.

NUTRITIONAL ANALYSIS

SERVING SIZE: 2 eggs, 1 cup sauce, 1 pita bread, and ¼ cup yogurt (352 g)

PER SERVING: 420 calories; 12 g fat; 28 g protein; 56 g carbohydrate; 10 g dietary fiber

CHAPTER 6

10 Snacks and Treats in 20 Minutes

From crunchy to savory to sweet, these snacks are perfect for curbing breakthrough hunger, boosting energy levels, and meeting those tricky protein and fiber goals. The key question to ask yourself: Am I hungry, or am I reaching for this food out of habit, emotions, or boredom?

Although some people swear by their pre-workout snacks, others prefer to exercise on an empty stomach. If your goal is to optimize energy and muscle performance, a strategic pre-workout snack can be a game changer. But if you feel fine training between your usual meal periods, listen to your body and do what works for you!

SMOKED TROUT BITES

YIELD:
1 SERVING

PREP TIME:
5 MINUTES

Tinned fish is having a moment right now, and for good reason: it's an inexpensive way to get some quality protein. The best tinned fish come from Portugal or Spain, but you can pick up a tin or two right at your hometown grocery store. Smoked trout will be the closest to a more familiar fish such as tuna, but you can experiment with sardines, mackerel, or even smoked oysters.

¼ cup (36 g) nonfat cottage cheese
¼ teaspoon salt
⅛ teaspoon ground black pepper
¼ seedless cucumber, cut into ¼-inch (6-mm) rounds
½ can (2 ounces, or 57 g) smoked trout
Fresh dill for garnish

In a blender, blend cottage cheese, salt, and pepper. Spoon onto cucumber rounds and top each with smoked trout and a sprig of dill. Serve.

NUTRITIONAL ANALYSIS

SERVING SIZE: 1 cup (171 g)

PER SERVING: 170 calories; 7 g fat; 22 g protein; 4 g carbohydrate; 0 g dietary fiber

NOTE

Want that traditional Florida vacation fish dip feel? Serve with pickled jalapeños, lemon wedges, capers, and chopped red onions. Need a little carbohydrate? Serve with saltine crackers!

PEANUT BUTTER AND RASPBERRY RICE CAKES

YIELD: 1 SERVING

PREP TIME: 5 MINUTES

Rice cakes get a bad rap for being tasteless or boring, but there's something about their incredible crunch that is so satisfying. They're not just for bodybuilders anymore!

¼ cup (36 g) nonfat cottage cheese

2 tablespoons (10 g) peanut butter powder

2 plain rice cakes

½ cup (114 g) raspberries

In a blender, blend cottage cheese and peanut butter powder. Spread cottage cheese mixture on rice cakes, and top with the raspberries. Serve.

NUTRITIONAL ANALYSIS

SERVING SIZE: 2 prepared rice cakes (141 g)

PER SERVING: 190 calories; 2 g fat; 12 g protein; 30 g carbohydrate; 7 g dietary fiber

DEVILED EGGS

YIELD:
2 SERVINGS

PREP TIME:
10 MINUTES

Aren't these always the first thing to go at a picnic? You can make them the traditional way with some mustard, maybe some pickle relish, and paprika, but why not jazz them up a bit and pick a different flavor?

---

4 hard-boiled eggs, peeled

¼ cup (59 g) plain nonfat Greek yogurt

1 teaspoon (5 g) seasoning of your choice, such as ranch seasoning, taco seasoning, Italian herbs, or curry powder

Cut each egg in half, reserving yolks in a small bowl. Add yogurt and seasoning to yolks and stir until smooth. Spoon yolk mixture back into egg white halves. Serve.

GLUTEN FREE

VEGETARIAN

NUTRITIONAL ANALYSIS

SERVING SIZE: 4 deviled eggs (129 g)

PER SERVING: 180 calories; 11 g fat; 15 g protein; 3 g carbohydrate; 0 g dietary fiber

PIZZA CHICKPEAS

These snacks can take on just about any flavor you desire. See below for variations.

YIELD:
2 SERVINGS

PREP TIME:
5 MINUTES

COOK TIME:
15 MINUTES

2 tablespoons (33 g) tomato paste
1 tablespoon (3 g) nutritional yeast
1 teaspoon (3 g) Italian seasoning
½ teaspoon garlic powder
½ teaspoon salt
1 can (15.5 ounces, or 439 g) chickpeas, drained and rinsed

In a medium bowl, stir tomato paste, nutritional yeast, Italian seasoning, garlic powder, salt, and 1 tablespoon (15 ml) water. Stir in drained chickpeas, making sure they are all coated in tomato mixture. Spray an air fryer basket with cooking spray. Add the chickpeas in one layer. Air-fry at 400°F (200°C) for 15 minutes, stopping to shake the chickpeas once or twice. Remove from air fryer, and let cool before serving.

VARIATIONS

- **Mediterranean:** 1 teaspoon (3 g) smoked paprika, 1 teaspoon (1 g) oregano, and ½ teaspoon salt; toss with ¼ cup (28 g) feta
- **Sweet:** 1 tablespoon (12 g) sugar, 1 teaspoon (3 g) ground cinnamon, ½ teaspoon cocoa powder, and 2 tablespoons (12 g) coconut flakes
- **Mexican:** 1 teaspoon (3 g) cumin, ½ teaspoon salt, and 1 tablespoon (6 g) chopped fresh cilantro
- **Lemon Pepper:** Juice and zest from 1 lemon, ½ teaspoon ground black pepper, and ½ teaspoon salt

NUTRITIONAL ANALYSIS

SERVING SIZE: ½ cup (246 g)

PER SERVING: 230 calories; 5 g fat; 13 g protein; 36 g carbohydrate; 12 g dietary fiber

FAUX PÂTÉ

- **YIELD:** 4 SERVINGS
- **PREP TIME:** 10 MINUTES
- **COOK TIME:** 5 MINUTES

Although undeniably delicious, chicken liver pâté is so rich that it might make your head spin (and belly ache). This version is lighter, with a smoky flavor from the paprika, and it's vegetarian! Serve with high-protein chips or sturdy veggies such as carrots, celery, or cucumber slices.

- **½ cup (58 g) chopped onion**
- **1 cup (198 g) cooked lentils (canned works well here)**
- **2 hard-boiled eggs**
- **¼ cup (28 g) walnuts**
- **2 tablespoons (24 g) nonfat cottage cheese**
- **2 teaspoons (10 ml) lemon juice**
- **½ teaspoon salt**
- **¼ teaspoon ground black pepper**
- **1 tablespoon (6 g) chopped fresh parsley**

In a nonstick skillet sprayed with cooking spray, cook onion for 5 to 8 minutes, or until soft and just beginning to brown. Transfer to a food processor. Add lentils, eggs, walnuts, cottage cheese, lemon juice, salt, and pepper. Process until smooth, 20 to 30 seconds. Transfer to a serving dish, sprinkle with parsley, and serve.

GLUTEN FREE

VEGETARIAN

NUTRITIONAL ANALYSIS

SERVING SIZE: ½ cup (87 g)

PER SERVING: 160 calories; 8 g fat; 9 g protein; 13 g carbohydrate; 5 g dietary fiber

BUFFALO CHICKEN DIP

YIELD: 6 SERVINGS

PREP TIME: 10 MINUTES

All the flavor of a plate of wings with a lot less mess. Increase the amount of hot sauce if you like it really hot.

- **1 cup (145 g) nonfat cottage cheese**
- **1 tablespoon (15 ml) cayenne pepper hot sauce**
- **1 tablespoon (8 g) ranch seasoning**
- **6 ounces (170 g) shredded cooked chicken**
- **3 or 4 ribs celery, cut into 4-inch (10-cm) sticks**

In a blender, blend cottage cheese, hot sauce, and ranch seasoning until smooth. Transfer to a serving bowl, and stir in shredded chicken. If you prefer a warm dip, heat in the microwave for 1 to 2 minutes. Serve with celery sticks.

NUTRITIONAL ANALYSIS

SERVING SIZE: ⅓ cup (77 g)

PER SERVING: 70 calories; 1 g fat; 11 g protein; 3 g carbohydrate; 0 g dietary fiber

CREAMY GRAPE SALAD

YIELD: 4 SERVINGS

PREP TIME: 10 MINUTES

This refreshing salad hits all the notes: tangy, slightly sweet Greek yogurt, the juicy pop of a fresh grape, plus a little crunch from the pecans. If you can find cotton candy grapes, their super-sweet flavor will blow your mind.

- **1 pound (454 g) seedless grapes (red, green, or a combination)**
- **½ cup (118 g) plain nonfat Greek yogurt**
- **4 ounces (113 g) reduced-fat cream cheese, such as Neufchatel, softened**
- **1 teaspoon (5 ml) vanilla extract**
- **¼ cup (48 g) sugar**
- **¼ cup (28 g) chopped pecans**

De-stem, wash, and dry grapes. In a medium bowl, stir yogurt, cream cheese, vanilla, and sugar. Stir in grapes, and top with pecans. Serve.

NUTRITIONAL ANALYSIS

SERVING SIZE: ¾ cup (177 ml)

PER SERVING: 270 calories; 12 g fat; 7 g protein; 36 g carbohydrate; 2 g dietary fiber

CAULIFLOWER HUMMUS AND RED LENTIL WRAPS

YIELD:
6 SERVINGS

PREP TIME:
10 MINUTES

Hummus is ubiquitous these days, and there are a million ways to make it. The cauliflower here will blend right into the smooth chickpeas and you'll never be the wiser, just like when Mom tried to sneak veggies into anything she could when we were kids.

---

2 tablespoons (28 g) tahini

2 tablespoons (30 ml) fresh lemon juice

2 cloves garlic, minced

1 cup (124 g) cooked cauliflower; frozen and defrosted works well here

1 can (15.5 ounces, or 439 g) chickpeas, drained and rinsed

1 teaspoon (3 g) cumin

½ teaspoon salt

In a food processor, blend tahini, lemon juice, and garlic until pale and fluffy. Add cauliflower, chickpeas, cumin, and salt. Process until very smooth, stopping to scrape down the sides several times. When you think it's smooth enough, blend it for another minute. Add water or more lemon juice to get a spreadable consistency. Serve with Red Lentil Wraps (See recipe on opposite page).

GLUTEN FREE

VEGAN

NUTRITIONAL ANALYSIS

SERVING SIZE: ⅓ cup (76 g)

PER SERVING: 130 calories; 7 g fat; 5 g protein; 15 g carbohydrate; 4 g dietary fiber

Red Lentil Wraps

Just like the homemade tortillas, it's pretty fascinating what you can make from such humble ingredients. Unlike the long and unpronounceable list of ingredients in most grocery store wraps, there are just two familiar ingredients in these!

YIELD:
6 TO 8 WRAPS

PREP TIME:
3 HOURS
(SOAKING TIME)

COOK TIME:
15 MINUTES

1 cup (246 g) dry red lentils

In a medium bowl, combine lentils and 1 cup (237 ml) water. Cover and soak for 3 hours or refrigerate overnight.

Place soaked lentils in a blender or food processor. Blend until smooth and pourable. Heat a skillet over medium heat and spray with cooking spray. Drop ¼ cup (60 ml) lentil batter into the skillet and use a spoon to gently spread out into about a 6-inch (15-cm) circle. Cook 2 to 3 minutes, until the edges start to pull away from the pan. Turn over and cook on the other side for 1 to 2 minutes. Remove from skillet and stack on a plate covered with a kitchen towel. Repeat with remaining batter.

GLUTEN FREE

VEGAN

NUTRITIONAL ANALYSIS

SERVING SIZE: 1 wrap (105 g)

PER SERVING: 170 calories; 1 g fat; 11 g protein; 30 g carbohydrate; 5 g dietary fiber

CHOCOLATE PEANUT BUTTER CHIA PUDDING

YIELD:
2 SERVINGS

PREP TIME:
10 MINUTES

CHILL TIME:
3 HOURS

Chia seeds are a nutrition powerhouse (providing protein and fiber), and they take on a delicious pudding-like consistency when combined with a liquid. That makes them a fun and easy dessert that is very customizable: Add some fruit or jam on top, or make it vegan by using a plant-based milk. Or, skip the peanut butter powder, cocoa powder, and maple syrup and stir in a scoop of protein powder (chocolate flavor, if you have it!).

---

8 ounces (227 g) silken tofu
¼ cup (60 ml) nonfat milk
¼ cup (24 g) unsweetened cocoa powder
3 tablespoons (45 ml) maple syrup
2 tablespoons (10 g) peanut butter powder
2 tablespoons (15 g) chia seeds

In a blender or food processor, blend tofu, milk, cocoa powder, maple syrup, and peanut butter powder until smooth, scraping down the sides a few times. Stir in chia seeds (do not blend). Divide between two containers (mason jars work well here). Cover and refrigerate for 3 hours, or overnight.

NUTRITIONAL ANALYSIS

SERVING SIZE: 1 cup (201 g)

PER SERVING: 250 calories; 8 g fat; 12 g protein; 36 g carbohydrate; 8 g dietary fiber

PROTEIN TIRAMISU

YIELD:
4 SERVINGS

PREP TIME:
20 MINUTES

CHILL TIME:
4 HOURS

This lovely dessert is traditionally made with ladyfingers (a type of cookie) dipped in espresso or coffee and topped with a decadent mascarpone cheese topping. We've lightened it up by using oats in the base layer and silken tofu in the topping. To keep to the nontraditional theme, we like to top ours with a few mini chocolate chips.

---

1 pound (454 g) silken tofu

½ cup (118 ml) unsweetened brewed coffee

1 cup (80 g) rolled oats

1 teaspoon (4 g) plus ½ cup (96 g) sugar, divided

2 teaspoons (10 ml) vanilla extract

1 teaspoon (5 ml) almond extract

⅛ teaspoon salt

FOR SERVING

1 tablespoon (6 g) unsweetened cocoa powder

Mini chocolate chips for garnish (optional)

Drain tofu in a fine-mesh strainer for 10 minutes to remove as much liquid as possible.

In a small bowl, stir coffee, oats, and 1 teaspoon (4 g) sugar. Set aside.

In a blender, blend tofu, remaining sugar, vanilla, almond extract, and salt until smooth.

Divide oat mixture evenly between four ramekins. Press it firmly into the bottoms. Divide tofu mixture evenly on top of the oat mixture. Refrigerate (uncovered) for 4 hours, or overnight.

To serve: Sift cocoa powder over the top, and garnish with chocolate chips if desired. This is best eaten within a day of making it; the texture may become watery if it sits too long.

GLUTEN FREE: Use GF oats

VEGAN

NUTRITIONAL ANALYSIS

SERVING SIZE: 4 ounces (194 g; without optional chocolate chips)

PER SERVING: 250 calories; 5 g fat; 8 g protein; 42 g carbohydrate; 2 g dietary fiber

CHAPTER 7

7 Smoothies and Sips in 10 Minutes

Staying hydrated is crucial for overall health and can help manage some side effects of GLP-1 medications. We are all aware that we should "drink plenty of water," but let's be honest, plain ol' water gets old fast. In this chapter, we will sip beverages for all occasions—electrolytes for fatigue, ginger for nausea, smoothies for low-appetite days, and mocktails for entertaining (when alcohol isn't aligned with our goals).

BASIC FREEZER SMOOTHIE

YIELD:
1 SERVING

PREP TIME:
5 MINUTES

Every grocery store carries an amazing variety of bagged frozen fruit combinations. It's almost a sin to not take advantage of the bounty and make yourself a smoothie! You can often find preportioned ginger in the freezer section near the fruit. Believe us when we say it will take your smoothie to another level.

½ cup (70 g) frozen mango
½ cup (70 g) frozen strawberries
1 cup (81 g) fresh spinach
1 teaspoon (5 g) grated fresh ginger
1 scoop protein powder

In a blender, blend mango, strawberries, spinach, ginger, and protein powder until smooth. Serve immediately.

GLUTEN FREE

VEGAN

NUTRITIONAL ANALYSIS

SERVING SIZE: 1 smoothie (1 cup [244 g])

PER SERVING: 200 calories; 1 g fat; 27 g protein; 24 g carbohydrate; 4 g dietary fiber

BANANA CHURRO SMOOTHIE

YIELD: 1 SERVING

PREP TIME: 5 MINUTES

Although soy milk has only slightly less protein than cow's milk, it definitely has more protein than almond milk, which is why we chose it for this vegan smoothie. Of course, your protein powder choice can make or break a smoothie, so make sure to find one that you love.

---

1 cup (237 ml) soy milk
1 scoop vanilla protein powder
1 frozen banana
½ teaspoon ground cinnamon

In a blender, blend soy milk, protein powder, banana, and cinnamon until smooth. Serve immediately.

GLUTEN FREE

VEGAN

NUTRITIONAL ANALYSIS

SERVING SIZE: 1 smoothie (1½ cups [375 g])

PER SERVING: 280 calories; 5 g fat; 19 g protein; 45 g carbohydrate; 4 g dietary fiber

MANGO LASSI

YIELD:
1 SERVING

PREP TIME:
5 MINUTES

A lassi is a yogurt-based drink that hails from India, where it is often made with fruit and spices that are native to the region (mango grows profusely there). This drink is soothing to the stomach and is said to aid digestion after a rich or spicy meal—something we can all use!

---

1 cup (235 g) plain nonfat Greek yogurt
½ cup (70 g) mango chunks
1 teaspoon (5 ml) honey

In a blender, blend yogurt, mango, and honey until smooth. Serve immediately.

GLUTEN FREE

VEGETARIAN

NUTRITIONAL ANALYSIS

SERVING SIZE: 1 lassi (1¼ cups [314 g])

PER SERVING: 200 calories; 1 g fat; 24 g protein; 26 g carbohydrate; 1 g dietary fiber

COLD BREW KEFIR SMOOTHIE

YIELD:
1 SERVING

PREP TIME:
5 MINUTES

Add kefir to the list of amazing fermented foods out there these days. It has a tangy taste similar to yogurt, and it contains calcium and good-gut probiotics. Medjool dates are a natural and fiber-full way to sweeten this drink, and their flavor complements the coffee and banana perfectly.

---

2 medjool dates, pitted

1 cup (237 ml) plain nonfat kefir

¼ cup (60 ml) unsweetened brewed coffee, cold

1 banana, frozen

3 tablespoons (21 g) hemp seeds

In a blender, blend dates, kefir, coffee, banana, and hemp seeds until smooth. Serve immediately.

GLUTEN FREE

VEGETARIAN

NUTRITIONAL ANALYSIS

SERVING SIZE: 1 smoothie (1½ cups [469 g])

PER SERVING: 400 calories; 10 g fat; 20 g protein; 68 g carbohydrate; 6 g dietary fiber

NOTE

If your dates are not soft, place them in a small bowl and pour hot water over them. Let them sit for about 10 minutes. Drain them, discard the water, and remove and discard the pits. Then proceed with the recipe.

GINGER CARDAMOM TEA

YIELD: 1 SERVING

PREP TIME: 5 MINUTES

COOK TIME: 5 MINUTES

When your tummy is upset, ginger is the best thing for settling it. Fresh ginger makes all the difference here, and if it is organic, you don't even need to peel it. Cardamom is the perfect pairing, but if you can't find it, just use ground cinnamon or a cinnamon stick.

---

1 tablespoon (6 g) fresh ginger (about a thumb-sized piece)

1 cardamom pod, crushed, or substitute cinnamon

Honey for sweetening (optional)

In a small saucepan, bring 1 cup (237 ml) water, ginger, and cardamom to a boil. Strain and cool slightly before serving.

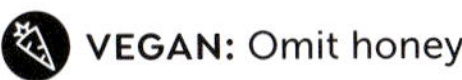

NUTRITIONAL ANALYSIS

SERVING SIZE: 1 cup (237 ml; without optional honey)

PER SERVING: 5 calories; 0 g fat; 0 g protein; 1 g carbohydrate; 0 g dietary fiber

MOCKTAIL MARGARITA

YIELD:
1 SERVING

PREP TIME:
5 MINUTES

Nonalcoholic liquors are widely available, making it easy to convert your favorite cocktail into a refreshing treat. If you don't want to buy a bottle of nonalcoholic tequila, just substitute seltzer and double the lime juice; it will still be a beach-worthy drink.

---

2 ounces (60 ml) nonalcoholic tequila

1 ounce (30 ml) fresh-squeezed lime juice

1 teaspoon (5 ml) agave nectar

Lime wedges for garnish (optional)

Sea salt for the rim (optional)

In a blender, blend tequila, lime juice, agave nectar, and 1 cup (237 ml) ice until combined and slushy.

To salt the rim of your glass, pour salt onto a plate that is wider than the glass. Run lime wedge all around the rim of the glass. Turn the glass upside down and place the rim into the salt. Carefully pour margarita into the glass. Garnish with a lime wedge, and serve.

 **GLUTEN FREE**

 **VEGAN**

NUTRITIONAL ANALYSIS

SERVING SIZE: 1 margarita (1½ cups [355 ml])

PER SERVING: 25 calories; 0 g fat; 0 g protein; 8 g carbohydrate; 0 g dietary fiber

NONALCOHOLIC SHANDY

YIELD:
2 SERVINGS

PREP TIME:
5 MINUTES

We couldn't leave the beer-lovers out of the fun! A shandy is usually a combination of beer and a citrus juice such as lemonade, making it a classic summer sip. Substituting a nonalcoholic light beer makes it easy to imbibe any day of the week.

---

1 can (12 ounces, or 355 ml) nonalcoholic beer, ideally Belgian or light ale

1 can (12 ounces, or 355 ml) no-sugar lemon-lime soda

Pour half a can of beer into each of two glasses. Top each with half a can of soda. Stir and serve cold.

GLUTEN FREE: Use GF beer

VEGAN

NUTRITIONAL ANALYSIS

SERVING SIZE: 1 shandy (1½ cups [710 ml])

PER SERVING: 60 calories; 0 g fat; 0 g protein; 14 g carbohydrate; 0 g dietary fiber

About the Author

Summer Kessel, RD, CSOWM, LDN, is a registered dietitian and certified specialist in obesity and weight management with more than a decade of experience, specializing in nutrition solutions and behavior change coaching for patients on GLP-1 anti-obesity medications. She is a champion for individualized, sustainable, and realistic nutrition and fitness interventions that improve quality of life and keep food fun. In addition to her professional skills, Summer has lost and maintained more than 140 pounds—of course, not without challenges—over the past twenty years, sharing her personal journey on social media along the way to build a community that encourages and supports others.

Her first book, *Living Your Healthiest Semaglutide Life: A Complete Guide to Nutrition and Mindset While on GLP-1 Medications*, was published in July 2025.

Index

D

E

F

G

H

I

J

K

L

M

N

O

P

Q